Run Elvin!

Gabriel Ndayishimiye

Copyright © 2021 by Gabriel Ndayishimiye

All rights reserved.

Run Elvin!

First edition: July 2021

ISBN: 978-1-7752442-7-1 (Ebook)

ISBN: 978-1-7752442-6-4 (Paperback)

ISBN: 978-1-7752442-8-8 (Hardcover)

ISBN: 978-1-7752442-9-5 (Audiobook)

This book is memoir. It reflects the author's present recollections of experiences over time. Some names and characteristics have been changed, some events have been compressed, and some dialogue has been recreated.

No part of this publication may be reproduced in any form, or by any means, electronic or mechanical, including photocopying, recording, or any information browsing, storage, or retrieval system, without permission in writing from the author, except in the case of brief quotations embodied in reviews and certain other non-commercial uses permitted by copyright law.

Cover Design: Gabriel Ndayishimiye, Liven Books

Editors: Rachel Joanne Macaulay, Tim Day, and
    Mary A. Metcalfe, MS

Dear Reader,

Thank you for supporting refugee authors.

Happy Reading!

Chrinthaly.

Gaby

FOREWORD

As you read through Gabriel's first book, you will quickly find out just how harrowing his life was at such a tender age. You will also see and feel, at the same time, all the emotion, passion, and integrity with which he tells his story! You cannot help by being swept up by it, and you'll want to finish this in one reading as I did.

I can remember the day Gabriel contacted me, just recently returned from academic work in Toronto, wanting me to read his manuscript, and all excited about his plans for a new publishing group.

When you finish reading this book, you will want to know more about the Rwanda Genocide of 1994 and why the world stood by and did nothing about it. This leads us directly to the question: how can we prevent more mass murder and ethnocide in the future? We have already been tested on that in Myanmar and have failed miserably.

But Gabriel is here to remind us that there is a way. A more gentle, peaceful way by honoring the people who came before us, who experienced the joys of giving birth and who gave us the breath of life and hope of freedom. Gabriel is on a road to express his love for that hope. Please join him on that journey.

> "I know there is a God
>
> because in Rwanda
>
> I shook hands with the devil."
>
> —LGen (ret) Hon. Romeo Dallaire
>
> Force Commander,
>
> UN Assistance Mission for Rwanda (1993–1994)

Kenneth Lumpkin
London, Ontario
3 December 2021

Dedicated to

My son Elvin Gabriel Jr.,

Rachel Joanne Macaulay,

Alyssa May Nunn,

and my father, a man I never knew.

In Memory of

My grandfather Joseph Ngerageze Karagita,

the only father I ever knew.

&

My teenage best friend

Henry Festus Ndayisenga.

> *"The stone, which the builders rejected, has become the chief cornerstone."*
>
> —Psalm 118: 22 (NKJV)

Elvin Gabriel Jr.

Born May 10th, 2017

CHAPTER 1

Son,

When you were born, I could not have begun to imagine how on earth I would manage being a parent. Now I cannot imagine my life without you, my loving and remarkable son. I named you Elvin in memory of your grandfather, the father I never knew. I think he would be happy to hold you in his arms, look into your innocent eyes and be proud to call you his grandson. You were born to be loved.

I hope you grow to find beauty in this absurdity, a journey that is your own life. I also hope you grow to embrace imperfections as you walk through this world, and as you work hard to become a better and more compassionate human. But who am I to tell you what your life should be?

My time is running out before I make up for all the mistakes I made. I hold regrets, like I believe we all do, and if I ever have the choice to go back in time, I hope to make things right; in a way, this text is that very opportunity. Any lesson I impart to you here, I pass on with love and the knowledge that you will be a better man than I am and better than my father was before me.

For every missed chance to show grace and wisdom I have missed, I pledge an honest and open-hearted lesson for you. I believe, our responsibility is not perfection but tireless growth. Each day provides us with a new opportunity to be the best version of ourselves, whether in earnest striving, failure, or triumph. That said, I hope you to learn to forgive yourself for not being perfect and that you do things that inspire you to create happiness in and for your own little world. Live not to anyone's expectations, including mine—especially not mine! There is no reason whatsoever to deprive yourself of joy in this life. You are who you are, and your individuality is a sacred right worth protecting. Self-acceptance and happiness go hand in hand. By now, I hope this you already know: you should never waste time putting yourself down. I repeat this like a broken record for a reason. First and foremost, it can be the easiest lesson to forget. These are words I never heard from my father and mother, who are far removed from the world I live in now. I learned all that I know from the filthy bars, showplaces, and dusty streets of refugee camps in Africa, and now from the sprawling, web-like metropoles of the 'First World'. I hope you can pass this message along to all your loved ones when the time comes. If you can't write, narrate the story once lived by spunky men and women. Strive for success but do not be ungrateful. Love yourself, your life, and know that all the little things that you might begin to take for granted should hold the greatest value as the first and last purpose in your life and endeavors. There is joy in all things for an open mind and grateful heart.

As you grow up and better yourself, you will learn that the simplest, most fundamental facts of your nature will make things difficult for you. Most of the time, this will not be your fault or happen because of anything you have done, but simply because of the way those with influence and privilege want the world to serve them.

But that is neither how the world works nor how it should. We, humans, form our world. That is, our world becomes what we make of it. It unfolds with each of our decisions, however small or seemingly inconsequential. We have freedom and possess the capacity to influence our social conditions and the conditions of those around us. We shape our own histories, traditions and beliefs, and our interpretation of right and wrong lies within our own consciousness, and through our projections of these interpretations into the world. This power of the individual, of each of our convictions, has echoed through society in countless voices before ours. James Baldwin's *My Dungeon Shook*—and Ta-Nehisi Coates's *Between the World and Me*—could not ring with more inspiring truth. Sadly, it remains true as I write these words that the world has not changed that much in spite of these messengers of change. I hope you mature to recognize both the benefits and limitations of growing up in the First World.

That said, I hope you will always be able to relate to people from all walks of life as you explore and learn from this world. I cannot wait to read your letters and hear about your experiences. My hope is that this letter and the pages that follow inspire you to be creative and strong in your own way. Never allow the storms of life or uncharted waters dull your passions or discourage you.

I have worked hard every day to offer you the future you deserve. I know that your life experiences are and will always be different from mine, and more than anything, I hope they will be so much better. But no matter how far you have come and will go, you need to know that not every moment will be sunshine and roses. There is no sunshine, joy, or glory without dark days of the soul for nothing good comes easy in this life. Goodness comes to those who go out and chase it, never to those who wait. Lucky Philip Dube reminds: *I can sit here and teach you every trick in the book, but at the end of the day, it is your life.*

CHAPTER 2

The lazy spring had finally done its thawing duty, freeing us from the icy grasp of Canadian winter. It was the beginning of my summer internship, in the office of the *Vice President, University Growth* at my school. My supervisor, thinking I might be interested, sent me an invitation, in a sealed envelope that began the long, winding journey that continues within the volume you hold in your hands today, wherever you find yourself along your own path. What I could not have known then, as I slid the letter out and unfolded it before me, was that this moment would prove to be a turning point in my life. The invitation read:

> Ten years ago, Kathy Mueller turned in her microphone as anchor of the evening news at CTV London and embarked on a humanitarian aid career . . . from flooded villages of Pakistan to small Indonesian

communities decimated by a tsunami, come and hear Kathy share her stories of survival and the motivation that keeps her going back.

As a student with global aspirations, I was eager to listen to Kathy's story. She was a veteran aid worker with experience in the tsunami reconstruction program in Indonesia and Japan. I was captivated by her years of experience working in the non-profit sector and by the possibility of hearing first-hand how her desire to help those in need had impacted the lives of others and shaped her own. In the story of a stranger, I could imagine where my academic goals and career aspirations might lead me.

My coworkers and I arrived at the venue right on time and were greeted by two hosts, who directed us to the buffet to serve ourselves. We made a toast to the Queen, and then sat to enjoy the meal. Kathy began speaking. She shared stories from the frontlines of crises around the world, explained the personal significance of each mission, and the continuing impact of her experiences upon returning to Canada. She talked about how aid workers, other practitioners in the field, and survivors can experience personal stigmatization—an unexpected, even paradoxical challenge—as they re-enter their home communities:

> The Ebola outbreak was the most challenging mission I have ever been on. I was having nightmares . . . there was so much death, I was going to more burials than I have ever been to in my entire life in Canada. Seeing the people suffering, that was really the toughest one to get through . . . so I came home for a resting period and people here did not understand Ebola, so they did not want to come anywhere near me. So, receiving that stigmatization was, well. . . that was definitely foreign to me. I wasn't expecting that at all.

In a moment of somber reflection, she paused and stared down at the podium in front of her. A heavy silence sucked the air from the room. My mouth hung open, stuck in a prolonged gasp at the notion of this cruel reality; I looked around and realized I was not alone. Everyone was completely shocked.

With a sigh, she looked up at us, over our empty lunch plates, almost apologetic for revealing the pain of her experience, and took a sip of water before continuing. She went on to tell the story of a little girl who was infected with Ebola, explaining how the girl was quickly checked into a treatment center and received the care she needed to recover fully in the following weeks.

In the course of time, the two developed a close relationship. However, due to the nature of the girl's condition, they could only interact from a distance, waving and exchanging tired smiles from across the quarantine barriers that separated them.

After completing medical checks and certified full recovery, the two were finally able to meet up close. They hugged and caught up on weeks of words unspoken across the barrier, having lived, in their own ways, through the greatest challenge of each of their lives. The girl was sent off to return to her family and a new beginning. Weeks later, they would be reunited in much happier circumstances: "She is a teenager now . . . has dreams to go to college to study law! She wants to be a lawyer and make her dad proud when she grows up."

She wants to be a lawyer to make her dad proud when she grows up. These familiar words echoed in my head with the profound but dream-like power of déjà vu. At the time, I recalled the challenges that African youth undergo to attain higher education. Opportunities to access higher education are rare and essentially out of reach for a majority of young people in most African countries. I know because I am one of them. Or I *was* one of them; my voyage to a university halfway across the world was one of struggle and good fortune in equal measure.

As you will learn within these pages, I recall every step with tremendous gratitude first, then a lingering frustration at the systemic failures that continue to make higher education elitist, capitalistic, and consequently inaccessible. Those who do get the opportunity to enroll at a college or university do not necessarily have access to quality education, either. There are too few institutions to accommodate the growing population and increased enrollment demand with each passing year. Beyond this, students who make it—and take on the financial burden of four or more years of tuition—find huge barriers to employment due to an overall lack of resources and opportunities upon graduation. For many African students and graduates, the scenario can feel like an unequivocal lose-lose; whether they take on the social and financial challenge of studying abroad or attend a university nearer home, they will be over-qualified for the limited job opportunities available to them.

Nonetheless, the tale of this resilient young woman cut through all my doubts and frustrations. A teenage girl, wisened beyond her years by adversity, dreams of becoming a lawyer to make her dad proud when she grows up. To a survivor of life-threatening illness, insurmountable odds are a plaster wall: dauntingly solid to the eye, only to shatter, hollow, under the force of sheer will. This statement of ambition and each breath spent to speak it is an act of great courage.

Kathy's words faded as I remembered my own childhood in the African continent. I was quite little in April 1994 when the Rwandan Genocide began its hundred-day decimation of some 800,000 citizens (about half the population of Montreal, as I type this). Two months later, my identity was no longer my own but got caught up in a historic moment. I, too, would be branded a Survivor, a title that somehow suggests both the eternal fragility and strength of humanity while also subjecting its bearer to millennia-old preconceptions in every culture.

I would spend twenty-two years of my life struggling in the confines of refugee camps across different countries in Eastern and Southern Africa. To these places and their people, my humanity was bound up in my status as a refugee. You know, it is a feeling of spiritual detainment, trapped not physically but existentially inside a perimeter, and parameters forbidding people like me the freedom to move, denied the opportunity that so many youths elsewhere took for granted: the pursuit of higher education as an indoctrinable privilege of being born in the right place at the right time. This, my friend, I will always remember.

To many, what happened next might seem like an answered prayer. My opportunity to escape came in the form I had long dreamed, as a chance to study at a respected university in Canada. That, to be sure, meant the end of my psychological imprisonment in the land that had repeatedly disputed my humanity, endangered me, and split my family into emotionally and geographically distant factions. That, in all certainty, would be a kind of rebirth or awakening, a claim to new life and belonging.

I would step across the threshold into my new home and cast off my unchosen identity at the door like a cumbersome winter coat, freeing myself from its unbearable weight. In retrospect, this bold step was only the beginning; the challenging work of carving my identity out of the labels and norms cast upon the body I live in continues to this day. But is this not a mission we all undertake in this life? The universal question: Who am I? Your journey to self-discovery will be your own, as so has been mine. I hope we both find solace and some shred of wisdom in the unfolding steps forward—and back—that I share with you here.

Kathy's presentation ended, and I snapped back to reality, still shaken by what I rightly suspected was an inflection point in the course of my life. As I drove back to work with my coworkers that afternoon, we had a verbose conversation, a reflection on her experiences. That feeling of change, of new ideas born in nourishing sunlight, descended slowly first and then in a rapturous wave over me. I had always wanted to share a story, a personal story about a life lived in refugee camps, on the soils of Africa. Kathy's story confirmed to me the stories I carried with me were important and worthy of exploring. Encouraged by her words and experience, I decided to step outside of my comfort zone, overcome my fears, and begin scribbling on the pages you now hold.

The very idea of drafting a book has been so daunting that it has followed me through many sleepless nights as I reflect on, write, and rewrite every single idea and memory that crosses my mind, hoping to achieve a truly unabridged, uncompromising memoir. Essays, perhaps! Through this process of reflection, I would like to think I gradually have gained an understanding of forces and circumstances that produced the tantrums and demons I battle with daily. Mine is a sense of self I have held, of course for so long, deep inside, but had never allowed myself to openly explore. I am beginning to understand the shining steel of that double-edged sword we call Survivordom, which has for the most part been a mark of the life I have lived thus far. This emotional and intellectual dive inward has led me to the following essays. You know, pieces of me that will forever thrive in my soul.

CHAPTER 3

The people of my generation were born during Rwanda's moment of collapse. Independence from colonial rule, however liberating, led the way to a perilous future on the tumultuous ground laid by a long and impactful history of foreign control. Seeds of divisions and hate—planted and watered by the hands of the Germans, then fertilized by the Belgians—sprang into a tangled mass of escalating resentment toward a once privileged minority. The fateful harvest of this hateful sentiment culminated in the 1994 Rwandan Genocide, a massacre of millions of innocent men, women, and children of the once privileged members of the colony.

 What happened in 1994 in Rwanda was incomprehensibly tragic to many, comparable to only a handful of horrors in recorded history, including the Holocaust at the hands of the Nazi Party and its collaborators; nonetheless, the social and political trajectory that led to the atrocities is, in fact, clear and comprehensible to the point of predictability. Thus, understanding the *how* and *why* of the Rwandan Genocide does not require rocket science or some equivalently nuanced examination. A look back to the history of colonialism and colonial state-sponsored officiation of the Hutu-Tutsi schism—the origin of a false ethnic distinction and the root of conflict among the Rwandans explains it all.

To subjugate Rwandans under Germany's colonial mandate, the Germans embarked on a mission to divide and conquer Rwandan society by building on existing political tensions between the ruling class and the working class. Unlike their colonial counterparts, who planted themselves in various corners of Africa in a constellation of settlements across many regions, the Germans were not very much interested in the creation of a unified but widespread colonial authority. Their plans for conquest were much subtler. They pursued collaborative governance with the existing local authorities, thereby running the affairs of the colony under the pretense of a semi-autonomous (and Indigenous) government. Even though they worked alongside Christian missionaries and other mercenaries, the common notion of a "civilizing" mission was just a pretense used to obscure and aid their true agenda, which, perhaps unsurprisingly, was purely economic. The primary goals were to extract natural resources and trade in profitable cash crops—namely coffee, tea, and tobacco.

Before paper and silver currency became standard assets in Rwanda, cattle held unmatched value among the Banyarwanda. Rwanda's economy revolved around "payment in kind" (the exchange of goods or services for other goods or services in a kind of social bartering system within each community). A cow gained was a golden ticket to wealth, status, honor, respect, admiration, and recognition in Rwandan communities.

After demolishing the local socioeconomic model of "trade in kind" bartering, labor became a pure commodity, paper and silver money became the paradigm (as well as a further cultural liability for the disadvantaged). Rwanda's economy was forever changed. To protect the new economic model, Germans planted battalions countrywide, their many guns pointed in all directions, ready to shoot—and to kill—anyone who interrupted or questioned their business in occupied territories.

To achieve and maintain a successful colony, they recruited anyone with social capital. They tasked each with a duty to facilitate colonial relationships, a calculated attempt to win the trust and loyalty of the wider community. Through this process, the Germans learned some fundamental principles that soon helped them implement ethno-governmental policies.

They would create a network of colonial associates by befriending the silver-tongued, charismatic, and influential among various communities of economic value. The chosen associates were religiously indoctrinated to believe in a Hamitic hypothesis, asserting that African 'civilization' can be attributed to racially distinct Caucasoid invaders from the north/northeast of Africa. Further and further, the colonized associates believed they were the closest thing to the ethnically superior white man and, by association, to the Christian God. They were led to think they had been chosen and called upon by this God to command their subordinates given the unique (pseudo)intellectual capabilities evidenced by their relative material wealth within their communities. They developed a sense of pride, superiority, and power over their subordinates. It was as if the colonists had granted them a new identity distinct from their cultural heritage. In time, this led to the development of three ambiguous ethnic tribes that did not exist before the encounter with Europeans. Neighbors of the same blood were made alien to one another at the hands of the German imperial machine. Additionally, the colonized associates were subtly oriented toward the personal mythology of individualism, which included all other cultural values of Western Europe that discouraged communism and all forms of social integration or equality. They considered themselves enlightened by conventional Eurocentric approaches to life yet were paradoxically imbued with the loyalist principles of obedience and subservience to authority. To reinforce this shift among the colonized associates, the Germans openly considered the "well-colonized loyalists" an elite class—members of the content Tutsi pseudo-ethnicity who posed no threat to Germany's colonial enterprise. In material terms, this class only stood to benefit from their support of their European overlords. The colonized loyalists were not only privileged to receive training in new techniques and tactics to accumulate wealth for themselves and their families but were also taught new ways of organizing a nation—based upon a Western-centric world view—that would further cement their new status.

By the time of Germany's defeat during the First World War and subsequent retreat from its colonies, Rwandans had already begun to doubt and question pre-colonial traditions and cultural practices. Distrusting pre-colonial kinships, the wealthiest worked harder to keep the wealth circulating among themselves. The Christians married Christians, the affluent married the affluent, and so on. The pagans and the poor were outcast and stigmatized for practicing their ancient rites—practices that were labeled barbaric practices for heathens and pariahs. The idealization of Western notions of superiority and modernity created more divisions and contentious feelings among the Rwandans.

The Belgians and Christian missionaries brought with them nothing but colonial wickedness under the guise of Christian morality, Western ideals of progressivism, a monopoly on the truth, and falsified scientific discoveries of racial differences among the Rwandans—all manipulative endeavors in the name of material exploitation. The already at-risk Rwandan traditions, cultural practices, and community ties were reconstructed to suit Europe's colonial evangelism.

In 1933, the brutal force of a new colonial governmentality was born. The Belgians instituted and rationalized a national registration system and issued identity cards—with assigned ethnic identities inscribed prominently on their faces. The one-time "socioeconomic" classes had officially become state-identified "ethnicities." They preached and seemingly believed that the Tutsi were a naturally superior noble class descended from the Israeli tribe of Ham. The promoted differences between the Hutu, Tutsi, and Twa were nose size, height, and eye type. Such racial classification policy used peculiar physiological variation among the people of Rwanda to create and promote a newly exalted racial consciousness—a frenzied *superiority insanity*—among the Tutsi elite and a demoralizing sense of inferiority among the Hutu. Through the aftermath of WWI and WWII, the Belgians favored the Tutsi minority until the Christian educated Hutu-elite could take no more of their insults. They envied and resented the Tutsi for the exceptional treatment they enjoyed from the Belgians. When the dawn of decolonization neared in Africa, the Hutu male elites took it upon themselves to assert their manhood. They set out to prove they were just as capable (if not more capable) of running the affairs of the Rwandan nation. In retrospect, the Hutu believed they were in fact the right people to govern in large part due their majority presence in the country.

The early 1950s–1960s marked a new era of pan-Africanism, a movement of educated Africans who demanded independence from colonial rule and asserted their right to run on their own, the affairs of their national states. Until then, the Tutsi elitist monarchy had enjoyed a lengthy and profitable romance with the Belgians over the lifespan of colonialism in Rwanda. The Christian missionaries who once played a large part in stirring ethnic tensions and canonizing Tutsi superiority began to withdraw from their teachings; the Catholic Church seized this opportunity to publicly oppose the widespread mistreatment of the Hutu.

By the late 1950s, the backing of the colonial establishment had stoked the flames of Hutu defiance to a new boiling point. The promise of social change was no longer a spiritual velleity among the oppressed; a marginalized and downtrodden generation was beginning to grasp the very real possibility of systemic change. On March 24, 1957, a group of nine "ethnic" Hutu Christian intellectuals, led by seemingly unhinged, pro-Western anti-communist Grégoire Kayibanda, published *Le Manifeste des Bahutu: Note sur l'aspect social du problème racial indigène au Ruanda*. The manifesto was a ten-page document promulgated to denounce the exploitation of the Hutu by the ethnic Tutsi. The report called for the racial liberation of the Hutu people from 1) the White-Western European colonizers and 2) the Hamitic oppressors, the Tutsi. With this, Kayibanda envisioned Rwanda as a single ethnic nation. He argued: "The Hutu and Tutsi are two nations in one single state . . . Two nations between whom there are no intercourse and no sympathy, who are as ignorant as of each other's habits, thoughts and feeling as if they were dwellers of different zones, or inhabitants of different planets." In addition to claims put above, the report called for agrarian reform that would abolish indentured servitude (*uburetwa n'ubuhake*), a reprioritization of the right to own individual property, and the establishment of rural financial institutions to aid farmers and advance agricultural development across Rwanda. As these ideas gained traction and the threat of anti-colonial revolt began to loom large, the Belgian government systematically abandoned its allegiance with the Tutsi elites and began to empower the Hutu out of fear of an outright coup.

Having posed an imminent and public threat to the Tutsi monarchy, Kayibanda and his collaborators were hunted. Soon enough, rumors spread that one famous Hutu politician called Dominique Mbonyumutwa had been assaulted and murdered by the Tutsi. The fact that these rumors were nothing more than media manipulation couldn't prevent the turmoil that would, in what felt like an instant, sweep across the nation. The Hutu sought revenge, killing thousands of Tutsi and declaring their fellow citizens a mortal enemy. These massacres set off the Rwandan Revolution of 1959, which toppled the Tutsi monarchy and sent King Kigeli V. Ndahindurwa into exile, taking with him all pro-monarchists as political refugees. By 1960, the Tutsi monarchy had entirely withered. From January 28, 1960 to October 26, 1961, Mbonyumutwa, whose apparent murder had been used to rationalize the revolution itself, served as Rwanda's interim president.

When Rwanda conducted its first presidential election on October 26, 1961. Grégoire Kayibanda appeared alone on the ballot. Ironically, he declared himself the winner and the first "democratically elected" President of Rwanda. The [quasi-] independence of Rwanda had officially begun. In 1962, the Belgians left the country and Rwandans celebrated independence for the first time in history. Like elsewhere in Africa, European influence over the nation still lingered in what would prove to be an equally menacing form, a *neo-colonialism*.

As "THE MAN OF THE CENTURY"—a king by a new name, a wolf in sheep's clothes— Kayibanda advanced his vision of a Hutu-dominated republic. As if he had earned the right to supreme power over his subjects—"*Les Membres du Parti*"—and Rwanda's Tutsi minority, he unapologetically named his political party "*Parti du Mouvement de l'Emancipation Hutu ('Parmehutu')*." He swiftly advanced toward his ethnonationalist vision of Rwanda.

Of course, his presidency and time in office were not simply an unopposed merry-go-round of power or a testament to the privilege of being the country's newest authoritarian. The pro-monarchy Tutsi elite tested and challenged his authority at every turn. For example, those who fled in exile organized their power and resources and founded the *Union Nationale Rwandaise* (UNAR), a conservative, pro-monarchy political party whose objective was to restore the Tutsi monarchy to its former state, before the dawn of "independence" and the prompt erasure of the status quo. The stakes for all involved were dangerously high. Mbonyemutwa, Kayibanda, and their colleagues were wary of any threats against their power and went to extreme lengths to fortify their new republic. A growing paranoia brought Kayibanda's regime into conflict with the Tutsi elite among his political lackeys and appointed local authorities, ultimately leading his jurisdiction to its demise at the hands of monarchy apologists in 1963; these political dissenters called themselves *Inyenzi* (cockroaches) for their ability to infiltrate Rwandan communities at night—unnoticed—and mobilize supporters of their cause. He embarked on a gruesome war with all those who posed a threat to his new government, killing thousands and thousands of Tutsi. As a result, about 300,000 Rwandans from the Tutsi "ethnic" group fled Rwanda as refugees and settled in Uganda and other neighboring countries.

General Juvenal Habyarimana, a former minister of defense, ascended to power in 1973 through a military coup against the incumbent President Grégoire Kayibanda. In 1975, he created the *Mouvement révolutionnaire national pour le développement* as the country's only officially sanctioned party. True to his nature, he ran a military dictatorship until a new constitution was approved by national referendum in 1978. Unsurprisingly, Habyarimana was elected to serve a five-year term as president and remained in the high office through two uncontested elections in 1983 and 1988. He was a master of hyper-masculine posturing, known for the physical prowess, arrogance, and showy bravado that earned him the title "Kinani" — a Rwandan word for "invincible." This cult of personality and all its attendant flattery served as a perfect complement to the unprecedented levels of brutal totalitarianism Habyarimana inflicted upon the region with impunity.

In 1987, political antagonism broke out between Habyarimana's government and a new generation of young Rwandan refugees from Uganda. It was a long time coming; memories of "back home" never left the minds of their parents, instead transmitting intergenerationally, like some trauma-borne genetic mutation, to an already exiled youth population with a justifiable chip on its proverbial shoulder. "Home sweet home" memories, fairytales of days past, became the bedtime stories of this displaced generation. By 1989, their thirst for a return to the motherland had reached a fever pitch. No force or totalitarian will could oppose their commitment to this cause. Their first unified effort asserted their right to peacefully return to their homeland on the basis of their political rights and civil liberties. In any case, Habyarimana's government hesitated to grant their request, these young men and women were eager to command repatriation to Rwanda at any cost. His denial of their peace-honoring request would soon push them to validate his dictatorial anxieties: in 1990, leaders of the repatriation movement proclaimed that a rain of bullets would surely make their cries of anguish heard, proving yet again the time-honored maxim that—unlike the soundest of diplomatic appeals—the roar of violence never falls on deaf ears.

After a final peaceful (albeit contentious) disagreement over the conditions of repatriation and the redistribution of power, the rebels organized themselves and launched an attack on October 1, 1990. This marked the beginning of a three-year civil war between the government forces and the Rwandan Patriotic Front. After nearly three years of bloodshed, the fighting ceased on August 4, 1993 with the signing of the Arusha Peace Agreement. This agreement was short-lived, falling apart almost immediately with the assassination of President Juvenal Habyarimana, who was shot dead in his private Falcon-50 jet near Kigali

International Airport. Since then, life stopped in Rwanda, the world changed—and left us all with wounds that will never heal until the next coming of Jesus Christ of Nazareth on planet Earth.

CHAPTER 4

I was born with too much curiosity and not enough courage. As a child, I was raised to believe babies were bought in small packages from the hospital. I would go on to debate this with kids of my age, and none of them provided me with convincing answers. I had questions—quite reasonable questions, I reckoned—about how babies were bought and sold in the maternity ward, but I was too afraid and shy to ask those who were knowledgeable, so I pushed all my questions aside and settled into a state of solitude. I did not know who I could trust to share my anxieties with, who would break the standard of deference to the family superiors I perennially feared. I carried these feelings and questions with me like oversized luggage throughout my teenage years. I felt that my family, with everything they had gone through and the conditions they were living in, had enough to worry about without having to deal with my problems. I hoped that seeking their guidance might actually prevent problems from worsening down the road, but I was afraid they would be disappointed in me if I showed them my youthful vulnerabilities. How could I just ask such questions from nowhere? Would they believe these worries were crushing me to the ground? There were no signs of a breakdown; I had become skillful in playing this tragic game inside my head. Besides, mental problems were considered a sign of weakness in my family and the world I grew up in. I never dared to ask. Fear ran through my life to the point I convinced myself that nobody would ever understand how and why I was suffering. For so much of my life, silence was strength.

Talking about family was hard until one Sunday (afternoon), when I had a conflict with a friend who claimed to know my father and accused me of hiding him from my peers. I was on my way back home from church with a guy named Paul and other friends. Paul complimented my clothing style, and I kind of felt happy—happy about myself, as any genuine kindness does. That feeling was short-lived. Moments later, he asked: "Who is clothing you? Is your father sending you money from abroad?" I didn't know what "father" he was referring to, so I asked him to show some respect and mind himself before he commented about my private life. In short, and in the sternest tone I could muster, I told him to take back his words. He didn't know me! My closest friends, who knew me better and had earned such familiarity, knew I avoided conversations about my father, mother, and the rest of my family; I simply never told them anything so personal or intimate about my life. I was particularly sensitive to these types of discussions—especially in a public setting such as this—for reasons you will come to understand. When Paul mentioned my father, with the audacity to pretend to know me better than I knew myself, I was understandably angry. His reaction was shock—about my defensive reaction and change in mood. Refusing to let go of what I had all but implored him to avoid, he continued: "Stop being childish, Gabriel. Who doesn't know your father is in Belgium?" Hmm, BELGIUM! In that moment, in spite of my rational nature, every fiber of my being urged me to hit him in the face, if only to close the topic and cool the hateful fire rising in my chest with each passing moment. If only I could release all the silent anger that I had hosted like Dr. Jekyll's monster, unwelcome but inevitable, for all those many years. An almost primal instinct rose up: *Show your anger, and it will be heard*. Was this urge to violence a reasonable one? Another part of me reconsidered. He was almost seven years older than me, stronger and in all likelihood a more experienced fighter than I was. There was nothing that assured me that if I did start a fight I would end up the winner—rather than still being emotionally hurt, then with a badly damaged face to match. Even though I had gotten into lots of fights during my early years as a teenager, I still feared them.

My friends noticed I was going to do something foolish, so one of them decided to change the subject to soccer match stories, successfully dismissing the whole topic and preventing the minor quarrel from escalating into a fight. I realized I was becoming angry for an unworthy reason and that, if unchecked, I would make some reactionary decisions that would take me bad places. Realizing I needed the space to cool off, I excused myself and walked a different path to my grandparent's place to avoid any more trouble. The topic and subject of my father was too sensitive to discuss because it forced me to face the secretive, oft-repressed dark side of my life. I still believed that I was alone in this world and that no one could possibly understand my feelings.

The following days were hard for me. I didn't sleep well. I decided to swallow my pride and set up a meeting with Paul to apologize for my reaction on that particular Sunday. He accepted my apologies without hesitation. I asked him if he could tell me more about my father, explaining that no one in my family ever talked about him. The guy was shocked when he heard I had no information or contact from anyone assumed to be my father.

He started to explain: "Your dad, Emmanuel . . . always calls some people here asking about your whereabouts and how you are doing. I thought you knew about this whole thing and that you talk to him on the phone sometimes. This is the reason why I said what I said to you that Sunday. I am sorry that I hurt your feelings."

I listened silently. He continued, "I myself have talked to him on the phone in the past—a few years ago, actually. He lived in Kenya before he joined his brother in Belgium. There are people who have his contact there. I can ask to put you guys in touch. Hopefully, you two can speak one day."

He asked me to leave him with my phone number so he could forward my contact directly if he had the opportunity. I was amazed and moved by this story, but it was still hard to believe. Also, I didn't yet own a phone for myself, so I told him that I would keep checking in with him on a regular basis.

Hesitant to address the issue with my grandparents and uncles in general, I decided things would just work out themselves one day. This was an illusion. It wasn't long before I decided that enough was enough. Wasn't I already nineteen years old? Should my friends be speaking to my father before I did? I deserved to know the history of my family—especially that of my own father!

It was noon, and I had just arrived home for lunch. When I entered the house, my grandpa was seated outside having a smoke, and I found my grandma in the kitchen preparing a meal. Without any hesitation at all, I called out to her.

"Mother?"

"Yes, Gabriel?"

"Who is my biological father?" I shouted. "And when are you going to sit me down to explain what happened for me to grow up on my own without a father?"

Grandma wondered if I was sure I was okay. This was not typical of me. I was disappointed when she said, "Your father is the man who raised you, so go ask him that question." I could tell from her eyes that she was disappointed too, but something else in her face revealed a deep compassion toward me; my past, my current life and upbringing, and my future had just met at a crossroads in these two simple questions. However, this did not stop me from asking yet another seemingly pedestrian question.

"What's his name?" I asked.

"Joseph," she replied, then repeated the name slowly to convince herself of an invented truth. "Yes, Joseph is your father. There he is, having a smoke right outside. Go and ask him all the questions you want."

I was shocked and disappointed in her, for she surely knew she was not my biological mother and that my grandfather Joseph was not the father I begged to know. I stormed into the kitchen. "The fact that I grew up calling you my mom and dad does not really make you my biological parents." Evidently, she took this as an insult. She told me our conversation was done and asked me to get out of the kitchen, leave her alone, and mind my business. If the truth about my father wasn't *my business*, I couldn't imagine what was.

"I am not the person to answer those questions," she added. "go ask your grandpa and your uncles." But Grandpa had already overheard the last part of our conversation from the balcony and entered to figure out what was going on. Once he asked, Grandma was quick to respond: "Talk to your grandson here. He wants to know who his father is, his name, and where he is located now." Upon hearing this, Grandpa excused himself: "I am sorry guys, count me out of this discussion. My apologies. I didn't mean to intervene." The old man walked back to his favorite spot on the balcony to continue minding his business.

I was horribly disappointed. I left the kitchen and cried in my auntie's bedroom. I began to think that maybe Paul was right. I could not find peace in my heart until I found out the truth about my situation. Paul had given all the contact information for the man he told me was my father, so I began doing my research. I searched Facebook to find matches, but there were many people with the same username and their appearances never matched the image of my father that lived in my imagination. My father was a muscular man with a big head like mine, a happier face but somehow more judgmental; in my mind's eye, he looked like me. Nobody met my expectations. I decided to go meet with a woman who Paul suggested might know something, but the woman did not have any information to share with me. I was at a dead end.

My last resort would be my elderly uncle who lived in town. I had a chance to pay him a visit and asked him if he knew anything, but he too said that he had no particular information for me. However, he did reveal that my father's name was not

Emmanuel. He said my mother had always told them that my father's name was "Elvin" but that she never mentioned his second name.

CHAPTER 5

My mother instilled in us a work ethic in the spirit of one of her favorite Rwandan aphorisms, *igiti kigororwa kikiri gito*: "a tree can easily be straightened out when it is still young." She used the saying to enforce, and perhaps rationalize, to herself and to us, a culture of strict discipline in the family. Her parental ethos revolved around a genuine belief that the early years of a child's life contain within them the opportunities of a lifetime. Thus, her preoccupation with my early development was fueled by a high-voltage concern for not just my immediate well-being but my entire future—embryonic, fatherless, imperiled. She would compensate for the absence of one parent by disciplining me with the strength of two. I felt the gaping hole that was left in our home by the absence of my father, a shadowy figure whose continued yet distant existence, real or imagined, hung like a specter in our home. I never heard my mother bring him into our conversation. Not once. I wondered what he looked like, and secretly, whether my features resembled his. Did it pain my mother to look at my face and see traces of him? I suspected so but never dared to ask. While she missed the man she once knew, I longed for one I never did, because all around me circled reminders of what, or who, he could have been.

I envied kids my age who lived in a full family. That is, the kids who had both their biological parents, mothers, and fathers, living under one roof as a happy family. They looked happy playing along with their fathers. There was Rodriguez, my childhood playmate who lived just two blocks, a stone's throw, from my dilapidated hut. He and his young brother, Babu, were embraced by their father and showered with guidance and love. Whenever their father showed up from work while we played they would run to welcome him with hugs and smiles. I could only watch, wide-eyed with envy. They observed and learned from a man whose entire being was invested in their happiness; I was left to imagine the phantom, nowhere in sight but always in mind, who would never come to find me.

I couldn't have been the only kid jealous of Rodriguez's family. The neighborhood was full of kids raised by single mothers. I bet they too watched this man and his boys walk hand in hand from work or school to a warm home and wondered why no masculine hand reached out to them or the women they had promised to love and protect. Us lost boys carried a shared burden, tangled in the same stories: many had lost one or both of their parents while fleeing from or fighting in the wars.

They each had unique stories to tell, many of which contained secrets even more heartbreaking than mine. Despite all this loss and the perpetual confusion, unable to understand the true complexities of our own fractured universe, we played happily together. We were kids. But Lord knows the anxieties that ran through our minds—the unanswerable questions that begged answers our young minds could never comprehend. Perhaps we thought the dirty puddles we played in would act as a baptism, and the harder we played together, the more our painful secrets would be washed away—or turn to dust in the stagnant air surrounding us. However, still, Rodriguez and his young brother would put us back in our place.

By 1998, a good number of men on our street had been recruited to serve in the guerrilla movement as soldiers, officers, or secret agents of the Burundian political movements in exile, the refugee camps in Tanzania. Back then, they held their secret meetings at our home. My stepdad, now a high-ranking soldier in the Burundian army, was one of them. He supposedly left his career as a doctor at a community hospital in Lukole Camp to become a guerrilla soldier and fight for peace and democracy in his home country of Burundi. When duty called, he left Mama with a four-month-old baby, my stepbrother, whose name, *Democratie,* is a memento of his father's righteous efforts.

Democracy was an ideal that many men, including my stepfather, wagered their lives on. In their hearts and minds, it was justification enough for their military pursuits; this ambition ultimately ripped them from the arms of their loved ones, leaving young mothers and their infants hungry, alone, and uncertain in conditions they couldn't rightfully have wished upon their sworn enemies and oppressors.

A few years later, a wave of hearsay hit our sunbaked neighborhood, carrying with it the red tide of blood sacrificed by the men from our block who had fought and died in their pursuit of liberty. One story that stuck with me, the purest tableau of the desperation that drowned my people, told of my friend's father, Nguesso, who jumped over a bridge into a lake protesting the brutality they faced in the battle ahead. These rumors disturbed my mother, who had already endured several lifetimes of suffering by the time of her marriage to this Burundian national who once promised her protection in the refugee community. Marriage was my mother's coping mechanism, both spiritually and practically. As a woman caught between war-torn nations, she was made helpless by circumstances beyond her control. What little control she had—in momentary glimmers of hope and self-determination—will never be known to me.

I grew up with all that was left. After battling through the horrors of the Rwandan Genocide, all she wanted was what all war-ravaged and desperate souls yearn for, the opportunity to begin again. What trauma had stolen, she needed to reclaim: a place to feel safe, calm, at peace. Some respite, however brief, from the existential dread that shrouded her generation like a toxic fog. It's easy to imagine how she imagined that place at the right hand of a man with status and connections. However, her newest safe haven had unfinished business to take care of. He was determined to fight for his freedom, which he considered synonymous with (or perhaps mistook for) his dignity. He was ready to shed blood—his own and his enemies'—to free himself and his people. Yet again, my mother was betrayed by her own expectations.

When we first entered the Burundian community, I immediately sensed a pattern of norms within the culture forbidding me, in no uncertain terms, to ever announce my Rwandan identity to any of the children I played with. In the early morning hours before he left for work, my stepfather would train me to speak in a *Kirundi* (Burundi's native language) accent.

"Gabriel," he called out my name.

"*Karame*!" I answered—the Rwandan way.

"No! Not again! Kid . . . listen. Please. Follow my lips," he said, disappointed. "*SAA . . . SABWE!*"

We practiced together for weeks on end—until he was convinced that I sounded like "one of them." My world had changed. My nervous system had to be trained to be aware of these changes like my life depended upon it.

There was a chant about a ritual slaughter, a slaughter of the innocent, often sung by kids on my street, mocking people of Rwandan descent:

> *Abanyarwanda n'Abagome* (Rwandans are heartless, a cruel people)
>
> *Bafashe ka ga hene* (They caught the goat)
>
> *Bagashinga iryinyo rimwe* (They slaughtered it mercilessly and without compromise)
>
> *Ibyo munda ngo HOKOOO! HOKOOO!* (They savagely uprooted internal organs, left them to rot all over the land)

I chanted along.

I suspect the chant had something to do with the savageness of the Rwandan Genocide and the consequent killing of the Burundian president Cyprien Ntaryamira, who was shot down with a surface-to-air missile as the aircraft carrying him and President Juvenal Habyarimana was preparing to land in Kigali.

Back then, we kids believed presidents were superheroes. The president was the most intelligent, powerful man in the land. When asked by an adult who we aspired to be when we grew up, the response was obvious. The highly ambitious (but not necessarily most intelligent) kids declared, without so much as a stutter for deliberation: *President*. Maybe they felt the helplessness I did and saw but one shining symbol to deliver them from it. Perhaps they equated power with safety, not yet aged beyond an unshakable Darwinian impulse. In any case, they couldn't have seen that Dassault Falcon-50, a chariot for two kings of modern Africa, power incarnate, reduced to molten steel and ash in the garden of the presidential palace.

The smart and otherwise worldly yearned instead to become medical doctors, while a few expressed interest in teaching. In most cases though, kids who had fathers with higher social standing professions said they would follow in their father's footsteps. None of us were interested in becoming farmers. We perceived farming as a profession of the wretched, the uncivilized. My playmates' animosity toward Rwandans appeared quite reasonable then.

I believed my mother desperately feared eviction from what seemed like a safe haven from an isolation unimaginable to me at the time. Life had gotten too complicated for her, and she was convinced marriage to this man was the only escape there was. I could tell she was going through the most difficult days of her life, though the gravity of her personal crisis didn't fully register with me in my youthful naivety. I was too young to feel real compassion and too immature to do anything to help. In moments of distress, she would say to me "*Iyo uza kuba undi . . .*" ("I wish you were somebody," e.g., somebody more helpful around the house). Even then I wondered what help she expected from a five-year-old child.

So, I witnessed and experienced all the misery Mama was going through, helpless to improve her situation or mine. Without a husband's protection to maintain her new national identity and status, she feared eviction from the refugee camp. Stress about her future and ours continued to mount. Her two young sons had yet to contribute poison or positivity to their circumstances, and she was biding time she didn't have, always haunted by her inability to sustain us until we might one day help to sustain her.

To quell the nagging questions of how we would secure food and safety, she got involved with another Burundian man with whom she eventually had her third child, my stepsister. As if coming to terms with a fateful cycle, she named my younger sister Destine. Soon enough, that cycle reached its next inevitable stage, and my poor mother was once again betrayed by her own wishful longing: the third man, like two before him, also abandoned my mother, leaving her even more vulnerable than ever and with another beautiful, fragile child.

She was alone again, without enough hands to carry the babies she had brought into this world, let alone enough food to sustain their hungry mouths. In a community that would never welcome her for being Rwandan, the depth of that loneliness remains, to this day, impossible for me to fathom. Even in relative safety and comfort, the ghosts of her past lingered nearby, filling every silence with what could only have felt like curse upon curse.

CHAPTER 6

To protect diplomatic relations, the government of Tanzania granted neither asylum, nor refugee protection to the people of Rwandan descent. To live in Tanzania as a registered (legal) refugee, individuals (asylum seekers) were required to go through a self-identification Census. The system disguised Rwandans. To survive occasional forceful repatriation, and to qualify for refugee status, many Rwandans forged new national identities. There had been multiple attempts at forced repatriation, but the country continued to receive more and more Rwandan refugees, most of whom were fleeing from Congo during the Rwanda–Congo conflicts of the late 1990s.

In 2002, the government of Tanzania held a press conference, warning all Rwandan nationals to desert the lands of Tanzania before December 31st, 2002. The refugees were given a choice: either repatriate voluntarily before the deadline or face forceful repatriation once it had passed. It was the first semester of my third grade of primary school. My uncle, who had then secured asylum in Malawi, sent his brother-in-law, Mutabazi (who at the time smuggled refugees from Tanzania to either Malawi or Kenya) to conduct us out of Tanzania by New Year's Eve. Such was the case for many Rwandan refugees. Those who had no money to leave the country took up loans from their fellows, promising to pay back their creditors "if God willed." My grandparents had enough savings from their local beer-brewing business to get us to the Tanzania-Malawi border.

In the weeks that followed, my grandparents paid us many more visits than usual. These meetings always happened over the weekends and early in the morning. I learned of our escape plans by eavesdropping on conversations between them and my mother. What I didn't know is that my mother was staying behind. When I asked her about it, she told me it would only be a brief sojourn.

Anyway, I was fascinated by our trip to Malawi for several reasons. I had heard rumors from my peers that Kenya and Malawi were worlds apart from what Tanzania was to us refugees. Too young and naive to understand what that meant, I believed everything I was told. I also heard my peers arguing among themselves about the truth or fiction of stories about footwear handed out freely and found among rubbish piles in Kenya and Malawi. At that time, I was charmed with sandals and fantasized about life in Malawi as an opportunity to wear as many types of sandals as I could. I was equally excited about a possible chance to take my first ever ride in a car. These were my dreams then, childish but full of a longing as emotionally real as any I've felt since. I remember two weeks before the journey; I stopped attending classes. Mom saw my excitement, and she warned: if I ever let the news slip to anyone, anywhere, that would be the end of our journey before we could embark. My days of thrilled fantasy would be finished, yanked suddenly awake from a beautiful, hopeful dream.

The other kids and I were trained in basic greetings and responses in Swahili right before we left. We were instructed to memorize the greetings *Jambo* and *Mambo* and how to react to each. They explained to us the contrast between the two words: *Jambo* is more formal and could be used to address anyone—it is the most general and acceptable greeting. *Mambo* was to be used only with peers, more like saying "What's up?" The response would be *poa*, which means something like "cool" or "not much". In case we were confronted by the police (or anyone else, for that matter) and asked "*Kabila gani*?" (What tribe are you?), we were instructed to answer: "Burundi!"

On the day of our departure, I walked to my godfather's place for a haircut at dawn. My mother was going to have a busy day, and I hoped to look and feel my best. She prepared pilau rice and beef for supper—the finest meal in the refugee camp.

In the evening, I posed for a final photo with my siblings, a keepsake for what we could only expect to be a long separation. Before parting ways with the only parental bond I'd ever known, my mother looked in my eyes with so much love—that nearly masked the tears that welled in her eyes. She kneeled to my height and hugged me so tight as if to communicate: *Son, it's not my will to send you away. The future has become uncertain for me. I live under the shadows of fear, hiding, hoping to stay alive to fight through the next day. I don't want you to grow up seeing me in such situations. Your grandparents have loved you so much, and they do not want to leave you behind.*

Even in my community, where goodbyes without expiration dates are so common, that day I felt the separation between a mother and child—it felt so deeply, it lodges within me, took up permanent residence in the part of my heart that I am not sure will ever fully heal. Softly, in her tender voice, she said, "My son, my young tree, always remember your mother will be crying if you grow up crooked." I didn't know how to feel beyond what I have expressed on these pages you hold. It must have been a hard decision to make, but in these types of circumstances, life often decides for you.

When darkness fell, my grandparents and I left Lukole refugee camp to spend a night in Rumasi refugee camp, which I only later realized must've been a more strategic position to begin our journey.

We slept on a white plastic sheet emblazoned with UNHCR in blue paint. A few more families joined us with their children. Memories of the life I was leaving behind ebbed and flowed behind my closed eyelids, interrupted only by grand fantasies about the rosy future ahead of me. The two versions of life battled in mind, and I couldn't close my eyes to sleep. By 2:00 a.m. everyone was awake and getting ready to catch the minibus to the train station. We all dressed up to blend into the night, the green forest and shrubs on our way. Mutabazi was waiting for everyone at a tucked away tarmac road. When we reached the tarmac, a Toyota pickup truck full of night patrol police officers sat waiting for us. Afraid to be caught, we dispersed in every direction, each of us scrambling alone through brush and dodging the high-powered flashlight beams cast out by our pursuers. Even as a young boy, the stakes were very clear in my mind: getting caught meant deportation back to Rwanda. My grandparents ran their way, and I ran my own way—as fast and as far as I could—with a gray sack full of clothes and a bowl of leftover pilau rice in a plastic bag. Not one child, however afraid, cried or shouted out. Perhaps we knew the circumstances didn't allow it. Those who were pierced and gashed by thorns as they sprinted and stumbled through the bushes cried on the inside, acutely aware of the consequences if they were to draw attention to themselves. I don't understand how we all complied, but we did what circumstances demanded.

This was my first experience with the urgency of "fleeing" in the most immediate and literal sense. It was only then that I could fully imagine the terror felt by my family and other refugees during their escape from Rwanda in the 1990s, when they resisted forced repatriation by hiding in the forests of Tanzania. In that breathless moment on the tarmac in 2002, I felt the visceral terror of what it really means to be a refugee just as they had, terrorized by the harsh realities of being nationless, propelled forever onward in flight.

We were still hiding among baobabs and thicket when the night sky softened into muted pre-dawn gray. The sun would rise soon. Unspeaking, we hoped the bush was thick enough to shield us when the light came pouring through. Slowly and cautiously gathering back together, we prayed for our ride to arrive before the sun climbed over the horizon. When the minibus did finally arrive, our elders—parents and grandparents—changed into their finest clothes. They were experienced chameleons. They seemed to have accumulated through painful experience the "know-how" to pass through the police roadblocks unnoticed. Who could've imagined ever needing such a skill? To survive to the next bus stop and railway station, we'd need to move in silence, never walking in groups or signaling, however slightly, that we knew each other. Until we reached our final destination, our most urgent priority was to avoid suspicion.

On the first day of our journey, we spent the night at the railway station in Tabora District waiting to catch our next train to Dodoma City. The train arrived around 1:00 a.m. and by 3:00 a.m. it was ready to depart. While on the way, a fellow traveler named Ncenga was visited by his trauma. He began to cause trouble on the train. Once train security reached him, he could not articulate his problems or respond to questions. Overwhelmed and unable to speak Swahili, he began speaking Kinyarwanda and pointing at all of us who were traveling with him. Our parents panicked.

Mutabazi was nowhere in sight; I presume he ran off to avoid the trouble sure to come.

Despite their own panic, our elders had the presence of mind to look for an escape route off the train while it was still in motion. When we began to decelerate, the other youths and I managed to jump one by one from the cabin windows. My grandparents handed me the sack full of clothes, my few remaining possessions, cracked open the window, and urged me to jump off the train. I leaped out and tumbled down the embankment unharmed. That marked our separation.

I rested in the care of the families that had managed to get off the train. When morning came, we reported to a nearby police station as lost Burundian refugees in search of refugee protection. We also reported how we got separated on the train. We lived at the police station for ten days while the authorities tracked down our lost families. After reuniting everyone, the Tanzanian government sent us to a refugee transit in Kigoma, where we waited to be transferred to Mtendeli, a camp for Burundian refugees. By the time we arrived in Mtendeli, I had caught malaria and was terribly sick for about a month. As soon as my condition improved, we resumed our journey to Malawi. It was early 2003, and it seemed to me, in my childish naivety, that the worst of our troubles must surely have been behind us.

CHAPTER 7

Upon arrival, we reported to Malawian immigration and claimed refugee protection. After a thorough screening process, we were transferred to a transit area in Karonga district to wait for our final relocation to Dzaleka, a refugee camp set up in Dowa, a small district located to the north of Lilongwe, the capital city of Malawi. The camp is about 40–50 km from Lilongwe, as close as any refugee camp gets to a major city; most are located in inhospitable, isolated, and barren spaces, unwanted remains of a country's allotted space on the map—best to be left wild, out of sight, out of mind. However, Dzaleka's relative nearness to the city is the only thing that makes it exceptional. Before being turned into a refugee camp, it had been "developed" for another purpose, not in spite of but *because* of its inhospitability: the facilities of Dzaleka had served as a prison for political opponents of Hastings Kamuzu Banda's dictatorship.

Wild stories were told about Dzaleka, many involving detainees left out overnight to be punished by the ruthless winter chill. Most would be found dead the following morning. Those who survived were set free. To earn your freedom, you had to prove that you deserved it. Although we would never face such deliberate and calculated cruelty, time would prove that we refugees faced similar odds. Another story centered around an old, abandoned meat grinder. Friends who had lived long enough to learn the grotesque history of Dzaleka explained to me that the device had been used to grind the flesh of prisoners before it was fed to crocodiles in the camp pond.

Then there were *Lowa*, evil spirits said to hover around the camp. In Chichewa, the Malawian language, Lowa means "to enter" and is generally used by the natives to welcome visitors. When you arrive at someone's house, you would excuse yourself *"odi"* (Hello there!)—to which the host would answer *"lowani"* (Come in). The story goes that Lowa would visit residents' homes at night and knock on people's doors. If someone mistakenly answered *Lowani*, inviting the spirit in, that person would disappear into the night, carried off or perhaps consumed by their unwelcome guest.

My family and I went through long periods of interviews and assessment before we could move into the camp. We pleaded our case desperately, practically begging to stay in a place that hardly offered sufficient sustenance, let alone even the humblest comforts. I watched my fellow long-faced refugees cower with intimidation as they were forced to provide personal information to the bureaucratic elites, who were empowered to make life-changing decisions about those of us at their mercy. Oftentimes, they made these choices without a trace of empathy or compassion for the lives they could either uplift or destroy.

Once cleared for residence, we moved into a mud-brick and grass-thatched house amid a dense cluster of other homes just like it. The place seemed susceptible to every extreme: it heated up with almost supernatural speed during the hot season and froze just as suddenly in the winter. The roof was perpetually leaky, and I would help my grandfather fortify it over and over again throughout wet seasons.

Christian churches were and continue to be abundant in Dzaleka (last I checked, there were seventy-seven active denominations), each populated by more pastors and deacons than followers. Many wanted to be pastors, deacons, choirmasters, presidents, or really leaders of any sort with a title to flaunt, so that they might wield some power over the affairs of their congregants. Thus, conflict over the misappropriation or brazen embezzlement of church funds became regular gossip in the camp. A simple dispute between two of Christ's pious followers—perhaps a deacon and an ambitious choirmaster—meant the formation of an entirely new denomination the next day. There was also a mosque, of course, though the disputes between Shia and Sunni Muslims were too bitter and ideological for neighborly gossip; their conflict, as yet unresolved, is beyond reasoning for those outside their faith, whereas petty power grabs and hands in the Lord's cookie jar at least *seem* harmless enough to most.

The Catholic priests at my church encouraged us to find beauty and happiness in the life we lived. They believed there was a "God" in control of history and that our lives would be mended one day. Alternatively, my grandpa always advised me to keep my expectations in check. "Life is hard and exhausting," he'd say, constantly reminding me that for people in our circumstances, steeped in the ugliness of poverty, fear, and violence, finding beauty in life is easier said than done. So, I grew up navigating the gray area between two versions of life, one defined by faith in the Almighty, the all-loving Father, and the other by an equally absurd "smiling despair", a trauma hardening in the cracks of my being that I struggled each day to glaze over and hide from the world.

My takeaway was that life could mean many things, dependent on where you find yourself in the world. It certainly isn't perfect: Refugees learn this the hard way, and it becomes necessary for them to internalize these truths of the imperfection of life. The realities of life hit us each differently, and opportunities arise in many different forms. *Someday life will get better*, I would comfort myself.

Despite being encouraged to dream big, the lack of means to reach or even test my potential left me depressed, disillusioned, and at times hopeless. I was raised by Christians, baptized daily in their particular brand of certainty, indoctrinated by blind faith in the justice and balance of God's green Earth, but there was no green now, only every shade of oppressive dusty beige spread in rows between glossy PVC tents like crops that will never grow, tents that reflects the life-giving sun skyward as if to say, *You have no place here*. Where was this God now? Why did He spare me and take my neighbors? How did He expect me to find solace in the divine plan without a worldly place to call home? These questions, uttered skyward to a silent void that never ends, not in any direction, became one with their answers—silence to silence, mine and His, bound together only by my existence and His absence, despite everything I was ever told to feel and believe.

I grew up into an outwardly happy teen, but feelings of emptiness dominated my inner world, hidden from my grandparents, teachers, and friends. The mechanisms I built to conceal them, however tightly constructed and desperately held, fell away in every moment of solitude. I craved my old life with my mother, but I knew well enough that was just another fantasy inaccessible to a boy in my situation. At home with my grandparents, I was what many would consider reserved and soft-spoken. I was silent when community members visited and never opened my mouth to speak unless spoken to. If I had something important to say, I spoke quietly and with all the practiced composure I could muster, as if finding a voice somewhere outside of myself where it wouldn't filter through the pain that threatened to choke it. However, when surrounded with my peers at school or on the playground, sufficiently distracted from my suffering, I was the loudest. In class, my name appeared first on the list of noise makers. It's strange to think how two such different people can be trapped within the body of one small boy. I think this speaks to the lengths your mind will go to protect you from what goes bump in the night.

In time, the residents of Dzaleka have adapted to the brutality and cruel history of the world around them. As I write to you, the camp resembles a growing city. It has become a multicultural society and even an excellent tourist destination for visitors

(Westerners for the most part) to the central region of Malawi, a testament to resilience in the most trying circumstances.

CHAPTER 8

Even then, I had a few Malawian friends from the surrounding villages who admired life in the refugee camp. The poverty that surrounded their compounds led them to believe that we, their refugee friends in the camp, were better off because of the monthly food donations that camp residents received from the UNHCR. Little did they know how circumstances turned around when this aid was delayed for reasons no one understood.

In pursuit of their dreams to live in the camp, these Malawian kids came to look for jobs that enabled them to—even just temporarily—seek overnight refuge within its gates. A few of them had worked with me at a local bread bakery, owned by a Burundi man named Nduwayo. I earned 300 Malawian Kwachas (MK) ($2 USD) at Nduwayo's bakery, as a weekly payment deposited in my pocket every Tuesday.

The hunger of inaction drove me to better understand that no one was going to look out for me. All those years in transition, away from the woman who birthed me, life had been my strictest and smartest teacher. I learned to be responsible for my own happiness and success, I had to. Even though my grandparents had tried their best to support me, at the end of the day I was left alone to take care of my own needs.

Of course, basic needs like food and shelter were my grandparent's responsibility, but anything beyond that was my responsibility. Whether it was replacing tattered clothing or building upon my minuscule collection of hygiene products, I was responsible for supplementing the barest necessities, and with that ability, my life was happy and complete. Other than that, it was good my grandparents helped make sure I was going to grow up into a well-mannered, disciplined young man. Their diligence with regards to developing my character is something I will always remain grateful for.

At the recommendation of my grandfather, Abdulrahman (Abdul), one of my uncles, sent for me to live with him in the city on consent that he would send me to school there. The third term of my Grade 6 was a week away from opening. My uncle's invitation appeared to me a life opportunity to escape the torments of life in the camp. He was a bachelor at that time and had thought I would get to help him in his grocery shop business while he ran business errands. Indeed, I proved a good asset, working long days in his shop. I helped him track down the supply and demand of goods for his grocery business. When it was time to start my third and last term of Grade 6, Abdul could not enroll me in school. I felt he failed to keep the promise he had made to my grandparents. His lack of concern and unmindful behavior for my future as far my academic development was concerned frightened me; I loved it at school. It was in school where I connected with lost memories of my mother, whom I left back as a primary school teacher. In school, I became a kid again, and any school's environment provided me with comfort and protected me from the outside world that forced me to grow up quickly. It was only in school where I commanded attention from both my teachers and classmates, all to assure myself I was worth something. The promises of gaining attention encouraged me to work harder in most of my classes, except Math. I always aimed to compete with the smartest kids in my class, and to keep among the top performers in class.

Yet I couldn't go back to school, I spent the rest of the term working hard, serving in my uncle's sweatshop, generating profits for his business. Weeks later, Abdul brought his youngest brother, Ali (another uncle) to live with us. Ali had just arrived in Malawi from Tanzania; we left him with close relatives the time we moved to Malawi. I thought it would be easier to talk to the youngest uncle about my concerns of missing out the entire school term. In fact, he also had to think about his future in regard to education. Coming to Malawi, he brought with him former class notebooks. He was a brilliant student I learned from his assessment notebooks and school reports. He indicated zeal to go back to school and, of course, Abdul took him away on a promise to send him to the best boarding Islamic secondary school in the city, Blantyre—until this never happened. With his education interrupted, Ali was brainwashed to believe in the empty promises of a brighter future as a businessman. How funny?

The whole term went just like that, and in January of 2007 I decided to take issues into my own hands. I talked to one primary school teacher who had turned into a regular customer at our shop, and he helped me register in Grade 7, but the school administration decided I must write a set examination to assess my fitness to be in at this level considering the fact I missed my third term of Grade 6. I passed all the exams, and started going to school again, a decision that did not please my two uncles.

One Monday, morning I woke up early to fetch water and sweep the compound. Diligently, I did all the household chores expected of me before I left for school. When I was in the middle of one of my tasks, Ali asked me to help him with "a little something," but I ignored him on account that his responsibilities were not mine to bear. I took care of my own issues. I thought it was quite reasonable for him to learn how to deal with his. My dismissal of his request is just one of the many incidents that indicated the decline of our relationship. It didn't strike me as much then, but now I recognize our relationship had become twisted, and a palpable distance grew between us, starting from the day I announced my return to school.

My discourtesies had reached a boiling point. We broke out into a fight. Faster than our fists could fly, or our legs could move, my fate was sealed: this petty warring between cousins was reason enough for my already disgruntled uncles to send me back to the refugee camp—empty-handed, deprived of the education they had promised me, with my head hung low as I presented myself to my grandparents as the guilty party of a pissing contest I had no desire to be a part of. My uncles forced me from their home like Satan cast out heaven. They gave no time to say goodbye to friends I had made over the short period I lived in the city. They allowed me to carry nothing but the uniform on my back—the one I had intended to wear that day to the school I would never step foot into.

Eventually, my grandpa conceded to taking me back to my former primary school to re-enroll me in my studies. I had no transfer or any paper proving I attended school in the city. The Headteacher explained it would be hard for me to get back into Grade 7 without any transcript or some sort of official note. Apparently, it was school policy that any student who did not report back to school after three consecutive months would lose their placement at the school. It's difficult to write this next sentence without evoking a sense of outrage at the betrayal of those who were supposed to be my guardians. The men charged with looking after me, my own flesh and blood, who denied my access to the one thing I valued most in the world, refused to send me the necessary documentation and, therefore, I had to repeat Grade 6. Despite their pity for my circumstance, there was nothing the school administration could do. Guiltless or not, I had to accept my fate.

I lived the rest of my young adult life mentally grappling with my separation from my mother and the drastic changes that consistently seemed to plague my attempts to live peacefully. I tried to blend into a world that would never give me the chance to live a normal life—a life that, to me, looked like Rodriguez and his little brother jumping into the arms of two loving parents.

I grew up quickly and took on responsibilities that were intended for a man well beyond my years. Constantly, I fought psychological battles to overcome the prejudicial conclusions people formed of me, railing against the false assumptions they formed because they failed to understand who I was beneath my half-crooked smile. I grew up tied to a merry-go-round that spun, without cause, in my young refugee world. As I lived within a small, stagnant bubble, the inaccessible world around me moved at the speed of light. I longed to step out of this perpetual spinning to become a part of the happenings that were far beyond the reach of a young refugee who needed to concern himself with how to get safely from point A to point B, not cultivate personal development or nourish the unfounded beliefs that something more was awaiting me—if I could just break out of this painful circus.

Today, I listen to all sorts of music (Reggae, Indie, Folk . . . name them). However, growing up, hip-hop culture spoke directly to my heart. Even though my language skills were poor at fully understanding the art, I connected with the messages and images I watched. They are many artists whose work inspired me, gave me hope, and kept me moving. Each evening, I would go sit in the corner of a nearby bar just to watch music on the TV screen. See, in my early years of primary school I was a drummer. I played our school's morning and afternoon drum, calling fellow students to attend Assembly. I had developed a great passion for drumming; however, this passion was lost soon after separating from my mother. A good drumbeat reconnected me with my stolen past. The elders wondered why I would be found at the bar, since it was not a part of our culture for underage kids to be there. In fact, most other kids would be in their homes, playing with their little ones, or their friends and neighbors in the compounds of their huts. No one would dare to talk to me, but when I looked around me, I noticed their strange stares. They would read from my facial expressions that I was not to be bothered. I did not judge them for their soothing libations, so my pacification, listening to music was none of their business.

Well, it was only my business to mind, until Mr. Moyo—my primary school Social Studies teacher—made it his. He had taught my class since he first arrived at my primary school in 2005. On this evening, Mr. Moyo found me seated comfortably at Michael's bar, listening to music as I always did. He did not talk to me, but out of shame I sheepishly walked out of the place I subconsciously knew was not appropriate for me to be in. Mr. Moyo had known me as a good student. I liked him as my teacher and enjoyed the subject matter he taught. He was a tough teacher, but his diligent teaching was softened by his kind treatment of us students. I had so much respect for him, and this respect led me to chastise myself.

    As I walked out of the bar, questions started crossing my mind. I don't drink, so what was I doing at the bar in the first place? Couldn't I find somewhere else to be than at the bar? Why couldn't I join my peers for evening stories, games, or whatever else kids should be doing at my age? Within this stream-of-consciousness, where I berated my poor decision-making, I realized how truly unbearable life was. I also recognized the unanswerability of, "Why me?" Did I deserve this pathetic excuse of an existence somehow—a life where a young boy was forced to seek refuge in a bar? This wave of self-pity contained within it much more important questions than those that begged why I had found myself here, and that question was, "How will I get better than this in this camp?"

The following day, after his morning class, Mr. Moyo called me to talk. "What were you seated doing at the bar, especially at that hour of the evening?" he asked. I wanted to explain, but he was quick to cut me off. He believed I had no reasons to defend myself. Instead, he started to give me some pieces of advice. I remained silent and listened to him. As we walked through the dusty earth walkway leading to the Administration and Staff Offices, we stopped to finish our conversation. He touched my shoulder and kindly looked into my eyes and said to me: "Gabe, you are a good student. Whatever reason you may have to watch music at the bar can never be strong enough to convince me otherwise. I want to see you make it to secondary school and become successful thereafter. Sitting at the bar and looking on as elderly men drink will coax you into following their habits at too young an age to recognize their consequences. These men have graduated from colleges and universities, and they are in positions to care for themselves and their families—privileges you have not yet earned. My hope is to see you grow up wisely and lead a good life, one that does not include barstools and lonely beverages."

The genuine nature of Mr. Moyo's advice was so intense I felt sorry for myself and for the direction my life was taking. I needed this advice—words of wisdom I never received from the phantom figure of my father. Leading up to this encounter and many times since, I always fantasized that one day I would encounter my dad in such a serendipitous fashion, and he would bestow upon me the care-filled advice Mr. Moyo had no obligation to share with just another one of his students.

***

I began my Grade 7 in 2008. Our class teacher, Mr. Misago, was a charismatic young fellow and taught science classes. He was very young for a teacher, the youngest in all staff members at school. We all loved him for this particular reason (we connected). We looked up to Mr. Misago as our role model. He was one of the successful candidates sponsored by the World University Services of Canada (WUSC) to study in Canada. He always encouraged us to strive for excellence. I remember the day of his departure to Canada, waving us bye from the airfield, and waving back from the visitor's lounge. That was my first day to step into an airport.

Anyway, so I was saying, during the second term of Grade 7, the World Vision International team distributed the English Standard Version of pocket-sized bibles. Their intention was to provide spiritual support for young refugees, the "we" who were disparaged by our circumstances.

World Vision International is one of those Evangelical Christian humanitarian aid, development, and advocacy organizations. You probably already know who they are from their commercials with all the distended bellies and the big, longing eyes of children from faraway lands. Well, prior to this interaction, I had no idea who they were because I was one of those underfed bellies and my forlorn gaze experienced the tragedies they attempted to portray in real life—not from the comfort of a couch through a television screen.

So, all students in senior classes at my school received a tiny Bible. I read it occasionally, before I went to bed. Mostly, I enjoyed passages about hope and faith that included things like "The LORD is near to the broken-hearted and saves those who are crushed in spirit." "He heals the broken-hearted and binds up their wounds." And, you know blah blah blah . . .!

I was desperate for comfort, and the promise my broken heart would at long last be mended—perhaps not while I wandered over hardened mud or clung to the walls of refugee camps, but maybe, one day, someone would find me worth healing—and have the pity and power to do so. Despite the consolation I got from reading biblical verses, the more I read the Bible, the more its teachings challenged me. It seemed everything I read was mythical and offered no practical solution to my very real problems. As much as they claimed otherwise, I quickly realized holy promises did not satiate hunger or provide adequate shelter, and the "Almighty Holy Father" could not fill the void of two lost parents. I sought answers from scripture, but they did not satisfy me: I constantly questioned why I was condemned to walk this particular path of life. I railed against the injustice of innocent young children being forced to carry burdens that even King David himself would cower beneath.

The final term of each class was the time to work hard and improve your grades if any student wanted to make it to the final year of my primary education, Grade 8. We were all under immense pressure, as we recognized the shame you would suffer from your friends if they progressed, and you were forced to repeat a grade twice: three repetitions were even possible—for the lazy or distracted student. The harsh reality, in my community, was that the ache of hunger, the loss of loved ones, and the challenge of sparse resources could not be counted as valid distractions from work or study because your neighbors suffered from the same plights alongside you, so your failures were never excused.

The transition from primary school to secondary school was a big deal to students. We heard so many good stories from friends—selected candidates who would leave the camp and go to study at these boarding schools. The feeling of getting out beyond the confines of the refugee camp was refreshing and provided temporary relief from the challenges that most students were experiencing. Good friends of mine reported back about all the cultural experiences and the much-improved morale on their campuses. Every teenager I knew was working to get a little glimpse of the freedoms and refreshment of living away from home.

I use *home* here with much reservation, as a refugee camp can never really provide the comforts you typically associate with that word. A camp may provide for your basic needs, but it certainly never nurtures you and you would never be proud to refer to that place of residence as the place where you lay your head at night.

The Jesuit Refugee Services (JRS) paid all tuition fees and handed out reasonable stipends to selected candidates. Despite JRS's efforts, parents worked even harder to save enough money to cover other costs, school-related expenses necessary to further their child's education. It was common practice that children who successfully entered secondary school were celebrated and revered by their parents and community members whenever they came to visit the camp. I can't articulate how intensely I longed for that escape and to experience, for the first time, the sense I was making my family—immediate and extended—proud.

However, when refugees from the former Ruwani refugee camp were transferred to the Dzaleka Refugee Camp, JRS decided to start a secondary school in Dzaleka to maximize the cost of funding of the boarding scholarships for refugee students. This news was extraordinarily unsettling to the 2007 Grade 8 cohort getting ready to enjoy the Promised Land of boarding school.

But the Catholic seminary exams offered a second chance to students whose parents could afford to pay the secondary school tuition and boarding fee. That's how Marie, my aunt, decided to sit for the Catholic seminary exams. Not that my grandparents would be able to pay for her education, but she was convinced that her brothers who then had successful businesses in town would compensate her expenses. And so, when the Catholic Student Seminar examination results were announced, she was selected to attend Ludzi Girls Secondary School (LGSS), one of the most prestigious single-gender educational institutions in Malawi.

Catholic schools in the country had a good reputation for reporting unprecedented pass rates during the national exams at all levels i.e., Primary School Leaving Certificate (PSLC), Junior Certificate Examination (JCE), and the Malawi School Certificate of Education (MSCE). Passing meant more opportunity and, for all refugee kids, the promise of opportunity simultaneously nourished us and kept us hungry, pushing us ever harder toward the ideal of a better life.

My uncles could not decide upon who among them would be responsible for paying her tuition fees. After a prolonged discussion, they come to the conclusion that everyone would chip in a certain amount of money to contribute. I, already well aware of the fleeting nature of good things, wondered where the funding for her subsequent years would come from—doubtful my uncles, who so vehemently extolled the value of education, would continue to use their precious resources to support my aunt's ambitions.

A day before my aunt left for school, I helped her get ready. I fried some snacks (peanuts and popcorn) so she could carry them with her, bought and packed Sobo Squash juice, and checked her bags to make sure she was all set for her journey. Grandma asked me to escort her to Lilongwe on the day of her trip, so I could look after her bag as she left to shop for the extra supplies she could not find at *Kagame & Diego's* grocery store. Kagame and Diego were two young brothers who ran their family business. Their grocery store was the most famous store in the camp, surrounding villages, and in the entire district of Dowa. In comparison to other major Canadian stores, Kagame & Diego's grocery would be the Walmart of our Dzaleka Refugee Camp.

I did everything asked of me and returned to Dzaleka after she had boarded a connecting bus to Mchinji. On my way back, Lord knows how much fire was burning in me after all I had just witnessed with my aunt's transition into secondary school. Right away, I set a goal to work even harder in Grade 8 to impress my uncles with my exceptional performance. I hoped, however foolishly, if they recognized my efforts and potential, they would sponsor my educational journey too.

I embarked on a habit of staying late to study and revise notes by myself and left usually before sunset when classrooms are closed. Madam Mukantumwa, the Vice Head teacher, usually left school late in the evenings after checking on the senior classes. These classrooms were kept closed to prevent little kids from messing with the subject matter displayed on the room's paper charts. Most of the time, she often found me in class, studying alone, and I would be required to leave because it was her duty to close each and every classroom that remained open. One day she recognized my hard work by giving me the keys to one of the Grade 5 classrooms, so I could use it to study every day after school. That way, she would not have to worry about disturbing my concentration or leaving the classroom open—it was a win/win (much more for me than her, as I was the sole beneficiary of her magnanimity).

In the second term, we sat for the Zone Mock Examinations, a standard examination meant to prepare us for the PLSCE national exam, and to promote competition between schools to determine the top best schools in the district. My school always came out first in the district. When the final results came out, my friend and I were at school, but we were anxious to listen to the outcomes of the Mock Examinations. Therefore, we all decided to go and wander in the bush in the area surrounding the school. However, despite the internal competition among ourselves, we reserved the top position for Eric—an extremely bright student—intelligent both within and beyond the classroom. He always got the first position, and there was never debate about how he would perform. We always said he was naturally gifted, but I think now, maybe that was unfair because when you say someone has a gift perhaps you threaten to undermine the tireless efforts they put into cultivating their abilities. But, giving thought to how your peers best you is not a priority when all you're thinking about is how their success pushes you further down the list.

Surprisingly, on this day, he was with the rest of our crew, perhaps to keep a low profile and, for once, to make his personality blend among his less *gifted* peers. With our correct presumption, Eric would secure the top position; the rest of us yearned and fought for second, third . . . Any spot with some notoriety or, more correctly, any spot that protected us and our loved ones from shame. Names were called out in our absence. The first position was obvious, second position was snatched up by Cyprien, the third went to Vincent, and Nathan took the fourth. But the position that really mattered to me and to you (my captive audience) was fifth. Because, that position was *mine*.

My grandmother did not have the opportunity to obtain a formal education during her youth, and she did not begin book learning until she was in her late fifties. On the other hand, my grandfather had made it up to Grade 6. He always had expectations for me to do well. No matter how hard I worked to improve, he was never satisfied. I wondered if both understood the pressures of formal education or comprehended the intimidation of examinations and all that I, as a young student, had to endure. I guess all they knew and recognized was every student had to work hard, as examinations were not easy and laziness in education often led to failure. Occasionally, we argued back and forth about my performance. When I tried to make him understand how much I was trying, and how circumstances in life were impacting my academics, they ignored my excuses and boldly claimed that it was my responsibility to work hard in class if I wanted to go far with my education. "We don't have any wealth—be it lands, animals, or property—in this refugee camp for you to inherit. If anything at all, school is what you have. Hold on to it. Be the best and do not just pass, surpass your expectations—and ours," my grandfather constantly chided me. I remembered these words whenever I had challenging examinations ahead of me. The examination days in school were never a nightmare as far as I was concerned. My only option was to succeed, and so I was always prepared with smart questions and got everything that was expected of me done on time.

A month later, *MANEB* announced the delivery of nominal rolls for the 2009 PLSCE. We wrote the examinations in three days: two exams per day—beginning Wednesday through to Friday. Meanwhile, the PLSCE national examination final results were just around the corner. I had all the confidence I would do well because I had dedicated as much time as possible to getting ready for these exams. I had, as they say, burned ashes to the ground with the sole purpose of convincing my uncles that, like my aunt's, my future was worth their investment. Unless the God I had read so much about had other plans, I felt confident my labor meant I deserved the glory and the crown.

A few weeks after the national exams, I joined other Catholic students who had registered to sit for the Catholic students seminary exams at Nanthomba Parish in Dowa. When I told my uncles about my intention to write this exam, to say they did not warmly welcome the idea would be a violent understatement. I needed 250 MK for registration. More importantly, I needed the 250 MK to continue to chase the dreams I had hungered after since I first became old enough to recognize the direness of my circumstances within the refugee camp. To put it in perspective, I was begging for less than fifty cents Canadian; yes, that's right, not even two quarters meant the difference between me returning to a life saddled up by the bar, staring longingly at music videos from socioeconomic stratospheres I would never, ever reach and a fresh start—outside the walls of a refugee camp where nothing, and no one, flourished.

To me, what these two quarters really stood for was the difference between life and a living death. My uncles did not recognize education as my only escape from the cycle of poverty that plagued my family for generations—and would continue to do so—should I not do something drastic to interrupt it. I was rejected by every single person I turned to for help. For once, I started to believe boarding school was never my destiny: I had foolishly allowed my hopes to blind me to the immutability of my circumstances and worked tirelessly toward something akin to a fairy tale. I turned to my grandparents, but they did not have enough money to enable me to write. They had been struggling to pay for cooking charcoal, cooking oil, and vegetables to supplement the food rations from the UNHCR.

While they struggled to compensate for our basic necessities, here I was, making exorbitant demands, adding weight to their already unbearable burdens. I recognize now how much this must have hurt them and how it may have seemed I was ungrateful for their love and support, which they likely never anticipated having to provide until the deterioration of my mother's ability to care for her children forced me upon their doorstep. However, as I've said, at that time—to me—education was synonymous with nourishment because I would have rather starved than swallowed the fact I would never have the hope of uprooting myself from the stagnant life of a refugee.

My world started to fall apart. For days I cried and cried, and I would cry again and pray to God in my bed, hoping He would turn things around. My grandma had tried her best to speak for me, but all to no avail. She finally decided to borrow money from one man named Konseye (one of the good businessmen in Dzaleka) on a promise to pay him back at the end of the month after the food distribution—she would agree to give him some kilos of maize, beans, or something as a payment for the debt. With this money, I finally passed another life trial.

But the money could not cover the fee, transport, and lunch, and so on the day of the exam I decided to walk to Dowa. After a week, the results were out, and Cyprien and I had scored the highest. Together with the other eleven selected students, we were asked to pay a second registration fee. The fee tripled this time. We were asked to pay 750 MK to sit for a final exam in Salima district. The final exams are used to determine school placements. Once more, I turned to my uncles for help. Pleading to convince them how much hard work I was investing in my education was not enough reason to give. As always, they all turned a blind eye on my performance.

We were given a period of two weeks to pay for the registration fee and be prepared to take the exam on Saturday of the third week. The first week—on a Sunday morning, names of the successful candidates were publicly announced in the church after the morning mass. The second Sunday, the list was not read to the public, but instead it would be pasted on the notice board or something. However, I was put to shame during the announcement period as the announcer singled out my name and called out loudly: "GABRIEL NDAYISHIMIYE is the only student who has not filled the form yet," he continued, "if the parents or guardian of GABRIEL NDAYISHIMIYE are here, they should meet up with the church council and to come pay for the registration of their student, not later than Friday— following week. Otherwise, the spot will be filled to a next potential student."

I wept and dried my tears where I was seated. I could not prevent stares from people who knew me. The murmurings around me were so uncomforting. I gave up my hopes for boarding school that day. I decided to stop thinking about it at all. I gave up all the boarding school fantasies because it became clear that I had no support. On Friday, the final day of registration, I was at home taking a nap when I heard my grandma's friend speaking in the house. I traced the voice to know who was speaking and then, it was Mama Elois. She had brought her the 750 MK.

Grandma woke me up and asked me to leave immediately and meet the church chair and find out if my form was still available. I ran the fastest I could and just when I was steps from approaching him, he saw me from my distance, called out my name, and said: "Gabriel, your form has been filled for Jean de Dieu." I was not terrified nor disappointed to hear this message. I had already given up and lost hope since. I returned home to explain this to Grandma. I thanked my grandma for doing her best. She had always been there for me and the thanksgiving for her was well deserved. That is what I could offer.

CHAPTER 9

When I started my Form 1 (Grade 9) at Dzaleka Community Day Secondary School, I held to my firm belief in the association between education and youth empowerment, and I desperately wanted to be involved in activities at my school. However, these early secondary school years were very difficult for me—and my pride—to endure. I was cognizant I looked different from my fellow students because I lacked a proper school uniform, which exacerbated my self-consciousness about being older than the majority of my peers. My grandpa had given me a pair of his black pants, which I appreciated. But he and I are not of a similar build, so the waist was too small, which meant the top button could not go up and my zipper was always only zipped halfway. I was frequently sent out of class by teachers who demanded I explain why I could not put on a proper uniform. Sometimes, I missed class periods to serve punishment because of my teachers' beliefs that I was willingly refusing to abide by the school's dress code. Every day, I felt insecure, not only about my hanging zipper and my ancient pants, which stuck out amid the sea of perfectly matching outfits. I was insecure I would travel all the way to school, only to be sent home by teachers who did not empathize with my situation. I knew my delinquency would only be tolerated by the administration for a limited time, and I feared the day when I would be expelled from class and refused re-admittance.

Throughout all of these humiliating interactions with my teachers and the students, who did not hesitate to point out my wardrobe malfunctions, I begged my uncles to send me money to buy the uniform. Finally, and thankfully, the elder brother took pity on me, sort of: he volunteered to send me one of his old pairs of pants and a shirt that aligned with the school's black and white uniform. The school also demanded we put on closed shoes, and my uncle was kind enough to send me his old pair of White Reebok CL Renaissance shoes. Everything sent to me was oversized, which isn't surprising as it was gifted from a man double my age and stature. But, at least, it was good enough to somewhat calm the tempers of the teachers whose last buttons I had certainly pushed with my nearly comical appearance.

Mr. Musafiri, the Headmaster, over-emphasized the importance of the school uniform policy and vowed to enforce the dress code on campus. The rules strictly regulated everything, barring even the most inoffensive things like holey hats and unkempt hair. The only exceptions were for hijabs or other outliers necessitated by religious and medical requirements. Certain students, who felt victimized by Mr. Musafiri's harsh leadership style, claimed he was heartless, so they bestowed upon him the nickname, Sulfuric Acid. Even though I myself had difficulties buying a proper school uniform, I was moved by the Headmaster's emphasis on the importance of proper dress on regulated school days. I observed all the students who had their uniforms on—they looked sharp. The thought of not having one—a properly fitting one—crushed me. One day, I decided to explain my situation to my late friend Festus. He told me I could use his pants and shirt, as he had a couple of each; he did not feel remiss in giving one to his unfortunately dressed comrade. From then on, I was finally able to share in the pride of wearing a uniform. From then on, I was happy, and more importantly for a young adolescent, I felt I fit in.

By the time I reached Form 2 (Grade 10), I was elected by my classmates to serve as the class monitor. And so occasionally, I would remain behind to supervise and clean up after classes. My classmates and I worked together to come up with a duty roster for cleaning the classroom. Our class teacher, Mr. Byiringiro, could never hide his appreciation, trust, and pride he had for us. He was the only teacher I have ever had, who openly reminded us that, *"You are all my little kids, and I love you all."* He was very inspiring to us. No wonder his name was *ibyiringiro*, a Rwandan language word to mean hope. His name signaled what a man he was. Very inspiring and loved by the students. Our final term of Form 2, Mr. Byiringiro held a party with his own money for the class. Mr. Chikwera, the Projector director, and Mr. Nyirongo, the new Headteacher and one other inspiring teacher Madam Mukantumwa were present. It was the first time in the history of that school for a teacher to hold a farewell party for his class. We loved Mr. Byiringiro.

The holidays were a good time to make money that would enable me to buy all the necessities I needed for the upcoming school year. Jobs were hard to find. A few days later, two of my friends—Elisha and Festus—told me there was one man who was looking for brick makers. Elisha and Festus were kind and said I could join them if I wanted. If I could make enough to buy a pair of shoes, two black pants, one white shirt for my school uniforms, and a winter coat, I would thank the heavens.

One evening, we had a meeting with the boss, Toto, the man who needed bricks. Toto explained he needed 1,000 bricks at MK6 each. The total would add up to MK 6,000, which would be divided among the three of us. "This deal is nonnegotiable, and you guys are free to start this evening if you like," Toto said, while leading us to a site where we would dig the soil and mold the bricks. The job took us about four days to complete—working from 5:30 a.m. to 9:00 p.m. We all congratulated another on our "good job," as the bricks were left to dry. By the time we finished, everyone had complained about low back strain. To dismiss this feeling, we blindly convinced ourselves that the money was worth it. After everything was in order, all work completed, we went to report to Toto.

"Good job, boys, that was faster than I thought. You boys are hardworking people . . . come back to see me in three to four days. I will pay you when all bricks are dry and after we have counted them. Hopefully, it will not rain these days, or the climate won't get too sunny, perhaps kids or animals will not damage them. As you know, we don't count any damaged bricks!

Disapprovingly, I looked into my friend's eyes—trying to communicate: *"This is the point where we beat him up to get our pay!"*

"This was not part of our contract, boss," Elisha said.

"Plus, you said you would pay us immediately after the job was completed," Festus added.

My friends turned to look at me, hoping I could add anything of use to defend our case. I had nothing to add. I gave the boss a look, the look I always make to emphasize my point. This was not a man to play games with. We knew him well! Everybody in the community knew how disloyal and untrustworthy he was. We accepted the job offer out of desperation. The second week came, the third week passed, and then it was nearly a month, and we weren't paid yet. With rage building up in me, I told my friends, if we don't beat the *hell* out of this guy, we should forget he will ever pay us. We should hope for the best because he had made his position clear enough.

Elisha advised us to report our case to the police and we did. Toto paid our money after being pressured and threatened with a jail sentence if he did not comply. He paid no compensation—if anything, we were thankful we were paid for our labor.

The summer holidays passed by quickly. The school year started in September 2012. I was now in Grade 11—the third year of my secondary school education. We were assigned Ms. Malongo as our new Class teacher. Leaving behind Mr. Byiringiro was bittersweet, but Ms. Malongo was another amazing teacher. In Form 3, my boys and I ran another successful campaign to represent my class, as the Class monitor.

During the final term of the school year, my classmates helped me with a campaign for the School Head Prefect position. I wanted to get involved as much as possibly I could. I thought by getting the role, I would be able to give something back to the school. I knew the role would require a lot of commitment and would challenge me in every aspect of my personality. As Class monitor, I was beginning to learn a lot about the value of collective efforts. My campaign was successful.

As a head prefect, my role consisted of being a role model for younger students to inspire them to be a good representative of Dzaleka CDSS. I helped with a number of events run in school, such as Open House day and parents' evenings, where I had to make sure that the school was represented in the best way possible. I also worked closely with fellow school prefects and class monitors to ensure students' concerns were heard and considered. Throughout the course of my term, I developed the ability and confidence to communicate with people across different age groups and this helped me a lot when I had to negotiate students' issues with staff members or when I had to motivate students to take part in school life.

The chance to make my ideas turn into reality, as well as the ideas of other students being heard, came about because I helped their voice be heard in school. Also, it allowed me to develop my public speaking skills, which I struggled with before I became a head boy. My purpose was to leave my school knowing that it was a fully accepting and safe environment, where all students were able to express themselves in the way they wanted and always be treated with respect. Since it was a mixture of people from different cultures and backgrounds, my ultimate goal was to make sure that the school was free from any form of bullying to ensure all the students developed their confidence to succeed in later life.

CHAPTER 10

The school years I had so earnestly coveted came to an end. As soon as graduation was over, I realized I had been irrevocably torn from the place that had nurtured my mind and character for the past several years. No longer would I be permitted time to grow within the safe haven that transformed me from a shy student in a mismatched uniform into the leader of my peers. While, of course, I was delighted I had graduated and proud of my accomplishments along the way, my very uncertain future in the refugee camp weighed heavily on me.

As time passed, and my friends began to get jobs and build upon the foundations of their lives, I became restless. On many occasions, one of my closest friends spoke of moving to South Africa. I was surprised by this because of the deep-seated fear many of my community members had of that area—talks of xenophobic attacks instilled a sense of foreboding in my family, and this was one of the reasons I could not follow my friend south. The other reason was the same one that shaped much of what I was ever able (or not able) to do: money. I didn't have the familiar connections or monetary wealth necessary to travel abroad and settle down somewhere else—somewhere with potentially more opportunity, more vibrancy and life.

My grandma and grandpa began to look at their lost grandchild with great sadness. They knew I was struggling within the confines of the refugee camp, but they had little power to save me or create space for me to save myself. Most of my classmates had begun successful businesses, others had found ways to overcome the seemingly insurmountable barriers to success our natural habitat created. I missed being a student. I missed my friends, learning, and the intermittent escapism attending class had allowed for.

After three months of this overbearing inactivity, my grandfather insisted I contact my uncles and ask for their help. He thought they could use my help in their grocery stores, even though my last visit had gone so terribly, and I had never taken steps to patch things up with them. When the reality of staying stagnant became more terrifying than the thought of reuniting with my ruthless uncles, I decided to reach out to them and ask if they would allow me to return to their city and work in their stores. I joined many of the young graduates in my village who said goodbye to the camp and went off to earn—not quite a living—but something like it.

Working for my uncles was not at all my vision for my life: there is little reward in stocking grocery shelves for very little money and even less appreciation. But, it was better than sitting in a bar in the refuge camping, sipping, and spending away time, and money, I certainly didn't have. What made it more difficult to swallow this new arrangement with my uncles was my inability to keep in contact with the people who really cared about me and my well-being. I didn't have a cellphone or a computer, which meant I didn't have any social media to stay up to date with what my friends and family were doing. At times, my uncle let me use their cellphones to access a Facebook account I could use to reach out to the people I had left behind. But, more and more, as I saw my friends' updates, when they shared posts and pictures of the progress they were making toward new careers and lives, I realized it seemed that they were, in fact, leaving me behind—not the other way around. I saw that most of them were working with Non-Governmental Organizations. They were doing things they were passionate about—things that mattered—meanwhile I was counting produce and contributing to my uncles' success, while doing nothing for my own.

In November of 2013, I returned to my refugee camp to receive the results of the MSCE. Here, I was surrounded by peers who were engaged with computer courses, the church, and charities that aimed to make a difference for kids like us. Their busy schedules left me on my own and accentuated my feelings of inadequacy. Being home made me jealous, and my envy of their progress caused me to question my life in the city and what would become of my decision to leave. I wanted to emulate their ability to take courses and prepare themselves for bigger and better things, but I knew if I followed their example, I would go back to drowning in poverty and the psychological and emotional benefits of intellectual pursuit could not outweigh empty pockets and foodless plates. But, despite this reasoning, I could not escape the feeling that I was missing out.

Eventually, I decided to apply to the Jesuit Commons: Higher Education at Margins (JC: HEM), seeking a scholarship. As part of the application, I needed to provide an analysis of their work in Dzaleka. Their mission was to identify educational needs in refugee communities to help marginalized children access learning opportunities that would empower them to break the cycle of poverty so rampant in this area. These courses helped kids to learn about entrepreneurship, enhance their English skills and encourage them to grow their understanding of other subjects that would give them the foundation for escape from refugee life.

Through this organization, I was able to apply for a Diploma in Liberal studies. In 2014, I was accepted into the program, which is forty-five credits completed online via one of the partnering universities in the United States. All of the courses are financially compensated for by donations and taught by volunteer faculty, so this meant I would not need to beg my family for the money necessary to take on this new milestone. I would enter the 2014–2017 cohort and, on October 17, received my official acceptance letter from Regis University in Denver, Colorado.

Thankfully, my grandparents shared in my celebration. I can only imagine how they worried if this chance I was taking would render me a great success or failure, but they unflinchingly extended their congratulations and affirmed my confidence I had done the right thing by abandoning my grocer duties for something more.

I wasn't satisfied with just becoming a student of the program: I wanted something greater. Through the Dzaleka Community Day Secondary School, you also had the chance to become a teaching assistant. To earn this position, one that I thought was honorable and rewarding, you had to successfully complete a formal application process. This included a form, cover letter, and in-person interviews that incorporated taking questions from a panel of interviewers, as well as demonstrating how you would work with small groups of students. Admittedly, I was intimidated by both this process and the job description that would follow, but I wasn't going to be deterred.

With my heart racing and insecurities pounding away at my mind, I met with the school's head teacher to find out my chances of securing such a prestigious position. He comforted me with the assertion that they weren't looking out for applicants' weaknesses, but rather to identify their strengths and get a better understanding of how they could contribute to the lives of the program's students. His reassurance gave me courage and the strength to believe I deserved this opportunity as much as the next person. I reminded myself of my academic standing, my work ethic, and ability to lead my peers, regardless of the circumstances I had previously found myself in.

I want you to read what I am about to say carefully because it is good for a young man to understand the difference between being humble, being confident, and being a fool. It is powerful to exercise humility and recognize your own shortcomings, but it is not right that you should limit yourself by pretending you are not good enough to try. This false humility renders humans useless because it allows them to give up while sparing them the guilt of doing so. It allows snakes to crawl into our minds and hiss, *you cannot do this* and poison us against ourselves and the actions we need to take to better our lives.

Overconfidence is just as deadly because it too prevents us from achieving success by allowing us to rest on our laurels and forgo the improvements we need to make in order to achieve things greater than we can imagine. So, my son, try never to become a fool—a man who builds up his own limitations and chooses to live in them. Instead, exercise humility, while also being strong enough to assert you are capable. That way, you will have enough drive to do more, without losing your head, heart, or soul. This too, this admittance of your weaknesses alongside your capabilities, is how you earn respect because it shows you are a human who works, and works hard, to earn goodness.

While we're on the topic of lessons, and I am making a habit of pointing them out—rather than giving you the space to figure them out on your own—I want to speak to you of discipline. My grandfather is the one who taught me the great study of discipline by always encouraging me to exercise restraint in all I do. He often reminded me that it is discipline, above all else, that helps a person achieve their goals—it is the necessary ingredient that transforms the hope for success into the real thing.

It's funny because, as I reflect upon the different values I hope to instill in you, I feel something akin to a chill. Maybe not quite that, but do you know when a person claims someone has walked over their grave? That is how I feel speaking to you, my son, about what I hope to teach you. Although I am far away from the stagnant refugee camp where little grew (including people) and so much was perpetually lost, I feel gripped with fear that I, myself, won't be here to teach you about discipline, respect, and endurance. Perhaps because I come from a fatherless place, it seems too good to be true that I will have the privilege of raising a son of my own. I need you to know it's a privilege I take seriously and, unless God Himself chooses to take me from you, it is one I will work hard to earn every single day.

Now, as I was saying—before I got distracted by the ruminations of a man who has so much to say and a nonsensical fear he won't have enough time to say it—I completed my application process for the teaching assistant position. And, a few days after making the acquaintance of the Headmaster at Dzaleka Secondary School, he phoned me to inform me I had passed all the necessary components and was being recruited by JRS to become a TA.

Little did I know how much this opportunity could mean to me. There is not a hint of hyperbole or overinflated positivity when I say I enjoyed every second of my experience. I was able to work with my former teachers, which was a great honor. Being with them again reminded me how much they had influenced my development; how much they had gone beyond what was required of them to do right by their students; and how much I was willing to do the same for my new pupils.

After months of interacting with my emotionally-void uncles, who were satisfied with menial work, as long as it meant good money, I was now in a place that prioritized learning and growing! I was surrounded by people who, like me, recognize that education is the medicine for most of society's ailments. Despite my demanding schedule as a university student and TA, each day I felt energized to wake up and go to work. What's more, my grandparents were so proud of me, and I was relieved I no longer pained them with the stress of my very uncertain future. Now, although I had not achieved great success in the monetary sense, I believe my passion and progress showed them I would not settle with a life not well lived. I would not go hungry, I would not sell my soul, and I would not remain within a refugee camp to live out the remainder of my days. These things, at least, I believe became clearer to the two people who cared most about me in the world.

CHAPTER 11

For once in my life, I felt as though happiness was blossoming all around me—green shoots of hope had somehow crept up through the concrete of my life and began to show promise of that intangible something I had always been running toward. These tiny sprouts took hold of my brain and my soul, lifting them, imperceptibly, to spaces they had not yet dared to go: places where things like safety, security, and success didn't perpetually evade your grasp, based solely upon your circumstances alone. It was a beautiful time for me.

But, I will caution you, son, that while hope ignites the soul and lifts the heart up, regardless of the weight it has borne, hope is also a very dangerous thing. It places the things you yearn for seemingly within reach; encourages you to stretch out your hand just a little bit farther, so you may brush the embodiment of your longing ever so slightly, with your fingertips. With each of hope's promises, you become more willing to suffer because you truly believe it will be answered by your heart's desire. And, like a siren calling lost men to sea, hope whispers in your ear that if only you can stretch, reach, and hold on for just a little bit longer, all will be well. But, sometimes, my son, hope is exactly that—a bait and hook that you don't realize is barbed with false promises and insurmountable circumstances.

You must be thinking, "Dad, you're so dramatic. Why the sudden change in pace when we've finally just begun to see the sunshine in this dreary story?" As a chiding smile creeps across my face, I whisper back to you, "Patience," because I fear your story, like mine, will ebb and flow: Sometimes, light will stream down upon you—you will be surrounded by love and inspired by hope. While, other times, you will be robbed by time, people, and circumstances, stripped bare of that buoyant, but duplicitous hope that raise you up to such a point where you became exposed to the elements, practically defenseless against an unforeseen change from peace to war. This fall from grace is especially difficult when you don't see it coming because, for once in your life, you unclenched your fists and your jaw, and believed you had earned the right to walk, uninhibited, toward your dreams.

This harsh lashing of reality hit me when I realized the thing that was bringing me so much joy may also prevent me from achieving my ultimate goal of creating a whole new life, far beyond the physical and psychological confines of being a refugee. While I thrived within JC-HEM, my eyesight had already drifted toward a loftier goal: to successfully apply for a scholarship with the Student Refugee Program (SRP) an initiative run by WUSC. This program was the only one of its kind within my camp—the only one that combined resettlement with the opportunity to pursue higher education.

Each year, SRP supports more than 130 student refugees to engage with over eighty universities in Canada in life-changing ways. These international partnerships create routes of escape from refugee camps and give young people a solid foundation in a faraway place to build a new and better life. Can you imagine what the promise of Canada sounded like? I don't know what your inclinations are toward music, but I am hopeful you will hear this as I describe it.

My ideas of Canada, planted like opalescent seeds rang out in my mind like the cautious, but impassioned strumming of a harpist with each tiny decibel of hope emboldening the next, until eventually a cacophony of potential rang throughout my mind in such a way it began to drown out my doubts and deafen my preconceived notions about what a life like mine was bound to sound like.

The pamphlets and SRP ambassadors spoke of Canada in such a way, it began like a myth — a promised land that the generosity of complete strangers was opening up to the hungry black minds that had been left behind by luck, location, and the undeniably discriminatory chains of pervasive, cyclical poverty. To me, Canada was built up to be a beautiful place where other young students would warmly welcome us into the safety, freedom, and opportunity that had been denied to us for being born in a country run ragged by times of trial.

Canada was the ideal and thinking back on the way I felt about it then, you'll notice, son, I cannot help but sound a bit like a man whose brain has turned to mush when he falls in love. But don't think I am crazy. Instead, try to imagine how quickly you'd be willing to give your heart to the promise of beauty and security when much of the rest of your life had always been tainted with the shades of violence and terror that spread throughout your communities and pierced their souls with a greater rapidity than any young man could hope to put a stop to. This is not that type of David and Goliath story, my son.

The more I learned about Canada and SRP's role in bringing young people, like me, there to learn and develop into individuals who had some kind of chance at something more than rations and sanctions, the more I needed to be a part of it—all of it. The application process for the 2016–2017 cohort opened in November 2015. I had all the required papers in place; I was ready. Actually, I was salivating: the chance I had longed for since I first recognized the inherent claustrophobia of refugee life was just a few dotted i's and crossed t's away. But eh, there's the rub—the cruel chafing of unrealized hope.

Much to my dismay, students already enrolled in the JC-HEM program were exempt from applying to SRP until they had completed the three-year curriculum they were already engaged in. Nine of us received this news like an unsharpened guillotine. We had all exceeded the academic requirements, produced the proper legal documentation, and demonstrated our commitment to community and positive involvement in extracurricular activities. We were candidates who seamlessly aligned with the mission and values of the program, and both my colleagues and the organization knew it.

But, rules are rules and, I will tell you this, there will be times in your life when, no matter how unjust something seems, you must simply hang your head and accept the circumstance. I know that sounds like weak advice for a father to give his son. It would be much more romantic to instill in you notions akin to those of epic warriors, of men who never hung their heads until they gasped their final breath. I wish I could tell you. But son, not every man's path can be beaten down; some of us must tread carefully toward the things that dreams are made of. And, don't you ever forget that your father did fight, but in a way that honored the time-tested statement that the pen is mightier than the sword.

I am writing this book, looking all around me—to the past and the far-off future, influenced by my current circumstances, memories, and yet unrealized plans for tomorrow. As I type this, I have no idea what kind of boy—or man—I am writing to. I don't know who you, my son, will be by the time you turn the first page of this heavy-laden adventure. But, an important part of this exercise is to give you little pieces of me that may help you become a better man.

So, I pause after the contradiction between the written word and the warrior to tell you the importance of cultivating knowledge and skills that you too can wield against the injustice I know you will, unfortunately, encounter at some points in your life. God willing, the adversity you face looks more like unfair bosses, rebellious peers, and small bouts of bad luck—rather than the seemingly insurmountable barriers of poverty, prejudice, and the other life-compromising offshoots of losing the proverbial geopolitical lottery.

My colleagues and I worked tirelessly to plead our case within a letter we hoped would move the hearts of the people who would determine whether or not I would get to see the *Promised Land* of Canada. Four letters were addressed to the WUSC head office in Ottawa; another went to the UNHCR Malawi Refugee representative and to the Protection officer; one was mailed to the JRS management, and the last letter was sent to the Dzaleka JC: HEM management.

To say I poured my heart and soul into those letters would be a laughable understatement, but now is not the time for laughter—because even as I sit here, within the safety of a place a far cry from the scared boy I was back then, when I think of the weight of that letter, I can feel it like metal chains tightening round my limbs, dragging me back to a place I have no business returning to.

With each of the letters signed, sealed and, God willing, delivered, it was time to turn my attention to ensuring my application was received. I knew that I could hand it in through the Camp Administrator's office, but when you are raised in a place where faith can, at times, be as scarce as the food, you quickly learn the importance of doing things for yourself. The odds were already piled so high against me; the thought of taking one more risk and trusting my future in the hands of someone else was like trying to balance a rock on top of a flower stem. I knew the only way I would trust that the application arrived where it needed to go would be if I hand-delivered it myself.

The kindness in her heart drove my grandmother to appeal to my uncles for money so I would be able to afford transport to the WUSC office in Lilongwe. If you can believe it, this time around, they reached into their shallow pockets and gave me what I needed to bus to the office and hand in my application. Back then, I was so caught up in the process of submitting this document, I don't know if I stopped to realize that this uncharacteristic display of my uncles' generosity meant that they finally recognized where I was headed—toward a future far away and far brighter than their own.

The letters were delivered, and the application dropped off, so now I would wait to see if the lady of fortune would choose to be cruel or kind. I know I've already talked to you about patience, my son, but let me tell you, the more you want something, the slower the moments drag by. The wait for a response to my pleading letters dropped by slower than thick honey off a cold branch. It's odd to think how, at the time, every minute seemed to contain one thousand more within it—like one of those beautiful little Russian nesting dolls, except none of these seconds, hours, or days were beautiful, and the burden of their gravity nearly suffocated me.

I hate to say that good things come to those who wait because that seems like something only old men say, once they've long surpassed their best before date and all their wisdom seeps out in pithy, superficial ditties. But, you already know this is true. After all of this fighting, I finally received the email that I, unknowingly, had been waiting for my entire life. The WUSC head office in Ottawa responded to our appeal and amended their policy so that applicants from the JC-HEM could be accepted into their student refugee program. You see, Elvin, the strategic pen (or for your generation, the keyboard) can be mightier than the sharpest blade.

In January 2015, I was called to sit for the written English examination to determine my eligibility to match with a Canadian university. Luckily, I did well and was able to progress to the next stage, which was the oral interviews. Again, by the grace of God, I passed. Each time I overcame one of these tasks, something cried out from the deepest part of my heart, "Thank you Lord God, for the love, the protection, and the gifts of wisdom and knowledge that have led me to this place."

However, while that part of my soul sang with joy, another part wept because I knew I was not the only one fighting to build a better life, and my name on that list meant another's had fallen off. And, not just a name, but the hope of a young person whose head would hang down low as they realized their chance for a better life had been snuffed out before the flame of possibility had really even had the chance to burn. I prayed for these students and hoped that God would give them the patience they needed to continue along their journey toward something better. I willed that they would find the strength and courage it required to take one more step in the direction of their dreams, but I also knew the toll it would take on them each and every time the glimmer of their dreams was tarnished by another rejection, another obstacle and another, "Not today, not for you."

I still think of those children, and I selfishly hope they ended up somewhere better than where I left them—I say selfishly because, in my mind, their success is as much for me as it is for them, so that I don't have to imagine that the fulfillment of my dream robbed them of theirs.

But, way back then, there wasn't enough time to mourn the loss of their opportunity; I had to prepare for the most important interviews of my life. Thanks to the JC-HEM, I was able to print my study resources for free, so I could read through each of the trickiest interview questions, over and over, until I started to run the risk of memorizing my answers and sounding like a robot, instead of a young man who wanted, so badly, to reach beyond the not-so-gilded cage of refugee life toward the very real, viable opportunity presented by a fresh start in a country where freedom is a right. The night before I would meet my proverbial makers, I couldn't sleep—all I could do was sweat, through my shirt and my sheets, until I was too hot, too cold, and too wet to even consider resting my eyes. However, fortunately, your father's sweating wasn't for nothing.

    My interview was scheduled from 9:15 to 9:45 a.m., so when the radio announced that it was 8:15, I concluded my breakfast with your great-grandparents early and began to collect my things to go. Before I left, I joined hands with my grandma, grandpa, and auntie, and we prayed that God would grant me whatever it is I would need to make the most out of those 30 minutes. It wasn't so much fear that clung to me, like those sleepless sweats, it was something more than that. I thought of my family, including my mother who was not there to squeeze my hand and wish me luck. I knew this interview was not just about me, and my voice was not only my own. I was going to speak on behalf of everyone I loved, and my success would be my way of thanking them for the sacrifices they had made to earn me that precious half hour.

As I prayed, I acknowledged the gravity of my opportunity: for, if I was successful, I would be the first person in the history of my family to access this level of education. I would be the first to step foot on Canadian soil, and likely the only who would have even some semblance of a shot at affecting the way the world works, rather than waiting four hours to fill a water bucket or resting their elbows on a dirty sports bar with a flickering TV.

I got lost in my thoughts, and the moments were not dragging by—they were flying. Everyone just stared at me, as I was rendered immobile by the realities that were crashing down upon me. I was running out of time, and when I came back to land, I realized everyone—except your great-grandfather—was crying. His eyes did not remain dry because he lacked sympathy for me; quite the opposite was true, he felt more afraid and sorrier for me than the rest because he knew I was stuck to that spot, and he worried if I had the strength to move. But, he did not show his concern through tears or sobs because that is not what he believed men do.

See, son, where we come from, the heads of homes do not get to be emotional. They must stand stoically and attempt to support those around them—like the pillars of a house, regardless of how shaky the foundation. I hope, by now, I have put an end to this example and that you know, when men cry, it is not a sign of weakness, but strength. It takes a very brave man to know he is still a man, even when he weeps—or, especially when. So, don't ever be afraid to show the ones you love how much they or the circumstances around them move you. I give you permission to be always exactly who you are—regardless of whether those emotions drip down your face or not.

Fortunately, my several minutes of overwhelming contemplation did not prevent me from being on time for my interview. After twenty long minutes of waiting, the interviewer called me into the room. I would love to tell you what happened next – that I gave perfect answers, and my judges applauded my efforts, but the truth is, I remember very little as to what happened next. But, what I will never forget is that on April 13, WUSC Malawi released the final selection list of those student refugees who would have the opportunity to travel to Canada. When it happened, I was working on an assignment at JC-HEM. One of my friends came running to tell me that the list had been released, and I was on it. Despite their excitement, I could not believe it. I thought they were making a cruel joke, so I dropped my things and went to see for myself. I ran my finger down the list and saw that two of my friends, Wycliffe and Bizimana, were named—and, as I am sure you have guessed by now, so was I.

I rushed home to tell my grandparents. Amid the celebration, my grandmother reminded me to thank God for this incredible blessing and for answering the prayers we had stood together and made that fateful day in our kitchen. While writing this out, I can hear the echo of Mathew 21:42, ringing in my ears – and in my heart, "The stone the builders rejected has become the cornerstone. This is from the Lord, and it is marvelous in our eyes."

Shortly after this brief, but honey sweet meeting, I ran to Wycliffe's house to tell him the news. As I barged into his home, I realized he was in the midst of making porridge. I knew this because he held a match in his hand, ready to strike and light his charcoal stove. When I told him that we would both be going to Canada, he dropped the box of matches and his cooking pot and started to jump around like a man who had gone mad. I stood back and watched, with a smile on my face, as my best friend lost his mind. After a few minutes, once he found it again, he said very casually, "Gabriel, the news is good." Wycliffe, always such a funny guy, using such a simple expression to convey the absolute transformation of our lives and everything as we once had known it.

Up until we received this news, it never really crossed my mind that perhaps, before, I wasn't really alive. I mean, of course I was living, breathing, walking, and eating. But, when I realized what I had achieved, it felt like my lungs finally fully expanded for the first time. The sense of relief almost pained me because the rush of joy felt so foreign.

I went from a young man merely putting one foot ahead of the other, to a person with real possibilities. Let me tell you, son, nothing fills your lungs or makes your heart beat quite like hope. I saw it in the other kids too—the lucky few who had, like me, been named on that list. We all came alive when we realized the rest of our lives would be lived somewhere far, far away in a place where dreams were not a foolish thing to have because food and safety are not resources as rare as precious metals.

My tireless efforts included months of training, refining my English skills so I could prove I was ready to leave Dzaleka behind and embark on my new life at a Canadian university. Each of us students completed a Canadian migration interview, and then we waited to find out at which university we each would be placed. Alongside my placement, I received a letter from Dr. Savino, a WUSC faculty adviser at Huron University in London, Ontario, who told me how excited he was that I would be attending his school. His kindness radiated off the page, and I felt so sure I was headed where I was meant to be—though I knew very little of my future school or what this very foreign country would hold for me. I guess it's hard to be afraid when your whole heart is bursting with excitement.

Although I would be leaving behind everything and everyone I ever knew and cared for, I was so focused on what was coming next, I don't think I ever really took the time to mourn what I was leaving behind. New beginnings have a way of overshadowing the ending of things; or, at least, that's what your father has found in his case. But, I will caution you, when you leave significant things behind and start anew, be careful to really say goodbye—because even if you return, the place you go back to will never be the same as you left it. And, even if certain things are painful or hold within them the suffering you experienced there, they still shaped who you are, and they deserve acknowledgment for that—if nothing else.

In August 2016, I left the refugee camp. It's still incredible for me to say that because it's so surreal. Do you remember when I told you about that one evening in the bar at the camp—when my teacher caught me in there and scolded me for giving the impression I was throwing my life away? I am not sure if I explained that evening well enough for you to understand how much sorrow I was filled with at that time. Because, when I watched that fuzzy soccer game, I was hopeless. I thought the farthest I would ever get would be stocking my uncles' grocery shelves with items I could barely afford to buy myself.

CHAPTER 12

So here I am, even today, feeling as though I am watching my life from outside myself, the main actor in a bizarre movie that begins in Rwanda and, by some strange twist of fate, finds me in Canada as I leave this trail of words, ideas, and feelings for you to follow.

It was a long time before I asked anyone else about my father. Almost two decades later, my mother told me:

> Son, your father would be proud of you. He would have loved to see you and see what you have become today. He seemed to be in his early 20s when I met him. We were both in our fourth year of secondary school at *Groupe Scholaire de Bicumbi* in Kigali, pursuing a career in *l'Éducation et Développement de la Petite Enfance*. He was quiet and reserved

talking to strangers. But when he opened his mouth to speak, he spoke with pride and confidence. Hardworking! He was highly ambitious and curious, just like you. I had no intentions of getting into a relationship at that time, but I fell in love. He was charming. Young and naive to grasp what love really meant for us—we found ourselves playing all sorts of games young lovers do. As the semester was coming to an end, I learned I was pregnant. This truth was too hard to bear. I wasn't sure how to break the "news" to my parents, my elder brother, and members of my extended family.

The clock was ticking. My time was running out before figuring out what to do with life forming inside me. I was terrified at the thought of being noticed. I ran away from long conversations and long stares from my female teachers and friends to the best of my ability. When I couldn't handle the guilt and shame any longer, I broke the news to my boyfriend, your father. He advised me to remain calm and collected. I followed his advice, and we were able to sit for our final exams without any suspicions from anyone in the school. It was time to go home for our *Grande Vacances* but before we parted ways, we promised to keep in touch. At the time, there was no access to "telecommunications", thanks to *des lettres postales* we were able to communicate—for a little while. When I arrived home, I talked to my parents—they were understanding and supportive.

   The following academic year began in September, and I was three months pregnant. I could not return to my old school in Kigali. Mom and Dad were able to enroll me back in school. I was enrolled in a private secondary school in my hometown. I studied harder despite my condition and finished my first semester with an outstanding performance. Your father kept his promise and occasionally sent me letters. I had love, care, and support all around me. I had all that I needed to make it through happy, safe, and healthy! The second semester of my fifth year of secondary school opened in January 1994. I was a month away from my due date. I could not go back to school, but initially, I had made arrangements with the school's administration to resume my studies six months after delivery. On the 15th of February 1994, you came into this world. I named you Liven Ndayishimiye (a combination of your father's first name, and my last name).

About two months later, we heard the announcement on the radio that the president's plane was shot down. At home, no one knew what was coming. We were waiting in fear, and then for a moment, I thought about your father where he was at school. That was it! It was over. People started turning against each other, and gruesome killings began. Students who made it home safely were lucky. Many of my classmates were targeted and killed. And your father? I don't know. I don't know what happened to him even today. I never knew anyone from his family. I have tried to trace him and failed many, many times. What happened was so acute, and nobody was allowed to scream.

We fled the country in June to seek refuge in Burundi, an identical-twin-nation to

Rwanda, a nation with very similar people, language, and past but divided with artificial borders and ethnic boundaries—to promote and secure the interests of colonial powers, of course. We lived in Burundi for about three months, and then extended conflicts in Burundi and Rwanda forced us out. We mixed with Burundian refugees and walked our way out of the country to reach the Tanzanian border after four days of starvation, sleepless nights, thirst, and swollen feet. We were led to Benaco, a refugee camp near the border of Rwanda. The geographical location of Rwandan refugee camps in Tanzania were said to cause political tensions between the new Rwandan government and the government of Tanzania. The new government in Kigali urged Tanzania to close down these refugee camps, claiming that they harbored *Génocidaires,* individuals guilty of the mass killings of the 1994 Rwandan Genocide against the Tutsi population.

In November 1996, Sergio de Mello, the Deputy officer for the United Nations High Commissioner for Refugees, in collaboration with the government of Tanzania, announced that the security situation in Rwanda had recovered. Ironically, the announcement encouraged refugees to return home voluntarily, with the expectation of having vacated the camp's premises by 31st December 1996. Refugees perceived this as a hardly subtle program of forced repatriation. By nightfall, a hundred thousand refugees had emptied out. Only the sick, starving, wounded, disabled, old, and otherwise weak—those who could not physically go any farther—remained behind. Those who had money in their pockets boarded minibus taxis and trains to Kenya and Malawi. No one in my family had money for such conveniences—least of all transport to a safer, more distant place where we could apply for asylum. We joined other refugees and stayed hidden in Tanzanian forests, sometimes moving from one refugee camp to another (between Musuhura and Rumasi), back and forth until the witch hunt stopped. In 1997, we joined Lukole, a refugee camp that was intentionally designated to accommodate refugees from Burundi. In 1997, I got married to Salvatore, your stepfather. In 1998, your brother was born—the same year you were baptized in the Catholic Church and were named *"Gabriel"* (your Uncle Alexis suggested the name). In 1999, I enrolled you in nursery school, and finally, in September 1999, you began your first year of primary school at *E. P. AKAZOZA.*

My mother's voice faded away, and I was immediately enveloped in a blinding rage over the loss of a father I never knew. What struck me most was the fact that when my mother lost contact with him, she had so little knowledge of his family or relatives that it's been virtually impossible to trace him. To make matters worse, she told me she never kept a single photo of him. She blames herself for all the mysteries of my life and for what her life turned out to be. I have learned to acknowledge these moments when they happen so I can offer assurance that all is forgiven. I am grown now, alive, and well. There's no sense in blame and guilt. Life is what it is. We have to carry on and live, to escape the shadowy clouds of our past into an always evolving future.

Though my words sound assuring at times, they are rarely enough to calm her down or convince her that things have turned out well for me. She is overjoyed by my academic successes, by all the comfort and hope I have found in Canada, achievements that are not mine alone.

I am learning to forgive my father, and to be equally kind to myself. It's been painful to have walked down this road without the fatherly support and guidance I so often idealize and require, but his absence taught me to be strong and get through tough situations on my own. Each day, I wake to the realization that you, my son, have filled the empty space that my dad left behind and filled my soul with a joy that I feared I might never know.

My life is like a movie. Sometimes I repeat these words to myself like a catchphrase, trying in vain to find some comforting frame of reference within which the absurdities of my situation could live without smothering me under their weight. I have learned that I am not the only fatherless child in this world, that there are countless more stories like mine, shared and unshared, each deeply personal and unique yet—in their common alienation—all the very same. At times, I try to reject this thought and carry on with life, but all attempts at blissful ignorance have left me hurting all the more.

CHAPTER 13

In February 2019, the Uniterra Program—a WUSC and CECI (Centre d'Etudes Canadien et de Coopération Internationale/Centre for International Studies and Cooperation) initiative—called for volunteers from multiple universities to participate in its 2019 International Seminar in Malawi. The purpose of the seminar was to bring together a diverse group of fifteen post-secondary students. The group was to be made up of five Canadians, five Malawians, and five student refugees living in Malawi. Together, these young people would learn alongside one another and deepen their collective understanding of issues and opportunities facing young refugees and host communities in Malawi.

When I found out about this opportunity, I was eager to participate. Not only did it align with my interest in working with my peers to address complex global problems, but it would also give me the chance to return home. Now, I am always grateful for my Canadian residence, my welcoming campus, and the comforts of living in a place like London, Ontario—a place so far removed from a village that held very little promise for me. But, for me, as I believe it may be for many refugees, the longing to be among the people, smells, landscapes, and sounds that raised you, never becomes drowned out—no matter how much your new circumstances wash over you.

But more than any familiar sight I missed, it was a brand-new one that I most wanted to see. And that was you, Elvin. No picture or video can ever do justice when a father has yet to meet his baby boy, and it has been a long time coming for me to finally hold you and count your ten fingers, and ten perfect toes. I am sorry I was not there when you were born, and I have become sorrier with each passing day that I have not been there to protect you and show you how much you are loved.

If you're reading this and you find me, yet again, far away, just remember that you, my son, will always call me back home. Now, I can't promise your home will always look as it does today.

Perhaps, as you're reading this, you are huddled under a blanket, fending off the biting cold of a Canadian winter. Or, maybe we will have found sanctuary, happiness, and love somewhere we have yet to even imagine. The location does not really matter though—for, no matter where you go, you will always be loved.

I must say, it's hard to stay on track with a narrative when your pen is in combat with such an outpouring of emotion.

I should not have kept so many of these thoughts and feelings bottled up for so long, and now I am here packing all of my fatherly advice into the pages of a book I haven't a clue as to whether or not will ever see the light of day beyond the bookshelf of my baby boy. But, that is neither here nor there, and I am getting in the way of reaching the most exciting part of this story—the part where I meet you.

After hearing about the volunteer opportunity in Malawi, I immediately made my interest clear, and once again, a combination of hard work, my experience, and good fortune came together beautifully to allow for me to see you for the very first time. But, of course, this trip cannot be all about our bond and much hard work had to be done to ensure the altruistic vision for the mission was fulfilled. That is, at the very least, when I feel I owe to my Malawian comrades, who did not make it across the sea, deserve—so one day too, they can write books to their sons with more happy parts than difficult ones.

The research process for the Uniterra Program went as such: students were guided by an academic adviser from a Canadian post-secondary institution and an academic adviser from a Malawian post-secondary institution. The seminar's theme was on "Youth Leadership for Refugee Self-Reliance" with the general goal of improving the lives of refugees who live in Dzaleka. These people include all my loved ones: my grandparents, my uncles, friends, and all those who contributed to raising me into the man I am today. Perhaps you will raise your eyebrows or crinkle your nose when you see your uncles listed among my desired benefactors after all you've read in this book about our trials and tribulations, but no matter what, they remain my family, and I still hold on to the thought that they truly did the best they could have, for who they are and how life had reared them.

On June 28th, my partners in this philanthropic research endeavor and I boarded the long flight to Malawi. What an interesting contrast between myself and the Canadian students. After living somewhere entirely foreign for several years, a place I had grown accustomed to and grown to love, I would be returning to a place that I knew like the imprints on my own hard-worked hands. On the other hand, my Canadian counterparts were leaving their homes, families, and all things familiar to become immersed within a community and culture that would be far removed from the close-knit campus of Huron.

We flew with Ethiopian Airlines all the way from Toronto to Addis Ababa, and then from Addis Ababa to Lilongwe. I was afraid on the plane; I thought maybe I would not make it to Malawi. While airplanes are said to be the safest mode of transport, at times they can be cruel. I am not sure if it was my contemplation of the technical ineptitude of the plane that frightened me, or perhaps I had just grown up to learn not to trust comfortable circumstances.

Throughout my lifetime, many things that were supposed to be safe and keep you that way turned out to be nothing more than snares disguised with an idealized cloth. But, when you're thousands of feet up in the air, with nowhere to go except in your mind, one can feel a little foolish exposing their apprehension to their peers—those who are happily chatting about upcoming adventures, breathing deeply as they doze off or snorting with laughter at an airplane movie you can't quite see. Despite my intermittent heart palpitations and the dark thoughts that threatened to overshadow the sunny day I could see glowing through the oddly shaped plane windows, I kept calm. Whenever those disturbing thoughts crossed my mind, I promised myself all was well. After a total of eighteen hours suspended in the air, we neared our final destination. I was meeting you the next day.

I arrived at Kamuzu International airport in Malawi around noon on the twenty-ninth. After methodically passing through customs, I looked around. I was immediately jerked out of the humdrum flow of the airport because, it was at that moment, I saw your mother waving. In her arms, she held a beautiful bouquet of fresh roses, but what stood beside those long red stems was far more captivating: it was you.

My young man, how handsome you looked! Without consideration of the people around me or the weight of the bags restraining my arms, I ran toward you. I sank down to hug you, unhesitating and overjoyed, and guess how you returned your father's embrace? You shrugged me off, pulled away and clung to your mother! I understand why you did this, how were you to know me from Adam? I tried not to take it personally, and I turned to hug your mother. While, after many long and lonely years, she welcomed the embrace, you—Elvin—remained obstinate. You would not allow me to even lift you up, let alone kiss or hold you. I was surprised you could not recognize me after I had called and seen you via WhatsApp so many times over the past years. But, despite my efforts to maintain our connection the best ways I could, you made it obvious I was a stranger to you. I tried again to carry you, but you wouldn't let me. The more I sought to be near you, the quicker you moved your little feet away from me.

I guess what makes a parent's love for their child different from the other types of love out there, is that even when it breaks our hearts, we do what we know is best for our children. So, although it made my heart ache to see you pull away, I understood you needed time to process all that you were witnessing. You needed time to get to know me, to get used to me, and perhaps to trust me. However, despite all that I was happy to have finally met you. But, I can tell you this, it is not right for a father to have to meet his son when he already has legs that can run away from him. My hope for you is that when you meet your little boy—or little girl—it is within that first instant they come into the world. I want you there, in that moment, holding the hand of your wife, wrapping your new baby in a swaddling cloth, and seeing exactly how miraculous it is to bring new life into this very strange, but beautiful world.

After I ripped my eyes away from you, my stubborn little man, I was more able to take in my surroundings. I was flattered to see my grandparents, uncles, and some family friends there to welcome me. After all these years, they were excited to welcome me home and hear all about my time in a place they could barely imagine. Unfortunately, it was not long before you and I had to slip back into the routine of being separate from one another, as I could not go home with you from the airport. My Canadian colleagues were waiting for me to drive to the Malawi Institute of Management (MIM) where we would be staying in the accommodations provided for us through the program.

While I longed to remain with you and your mother, and to make up for lost time, life seems to frequently tear us away from the things we love—or, at least, that has been my experience thus far. I had no time to convince you I was not a threat, but your father.

This bittersweet circumstance was all wound up with a tremendous opportunity I could not neglect. After all, I was there on a work mission, and I had to comply with the rules that guided my contract. Before I had to depart, I was given the time to take photos with you, your mother, and all of my other loved ones who came to see me. It was such a feeling to see their beaming faces. I wish I had more time to tell them about who I was becoming, so they would know their sacrifices and support had not been wasted. However, I take comfort in the fact that the smiles, captured within those photos, seemed to suggest they already knew.

I could tell the briefness of this encounter was felt by my family too. They were upset that our embraces could not last longer, and they would be denied a satisfactory update about all that I had been doing and what I was ripe to do now. Fifteen minutes is not enough to grab a snack, let alone catch up with everyone you've ever loved, under the iridescent lights of an overheated and unforgivingly public airport. However, we all found solace—me most of all—in the fact that now I was in Malawi, I would be able to use every moment of my weekends to spend time with all the people I had left behind to pursue my dreams of a better life.

Isn't it funny that my motivation to stay near to you and your mom had to be directly countered by my desire to build something better for us? Even as

I stood in that airport, I was nailed to the spot by my love for you and simultaneously pushed out the door by my commitment to Uniterra's mission and my promise to fulfill it. This mission not only represents my hope to make life better for all our people, but also to better myself—personally and professionally—so I may continue building the type of foundation that will provide you with security, freedom, and happiness.

I wonder if you will see that. Will you come to know that all of the moments I have lost with you, the distance that has prevented me from partaking in playtime and the reason I was nothing more than a man on a screen to you was all *because of you?* I hope so, because the alternative, the consuming resentment a young boy may have for the father he feels abandoned him, is too heartbreaking to even consider. I should know because so much of my life was infected by those thoughts. God help me if all my good intentions paved only a road to hell, away from the ones I love.

One day, I will ask you all these questions that, for now, lie merely as black and white blots on a speechless page. I pray you will have not only forgiveness but pride in your heart when we discuss how our paths crossed again. More than that, I hope not too long passes before they intertwine permanently. I think three birthdays is already too many for a father to miss, and I hope by the time you read this book, I have already made up for them.

But, we are nearly done, my son, so let me dry my eyes and move forward with the last piece of this convoluted puzzle, so we can go eat dinner, play catch, or do whichever activities you and I have grown to love together.

The next day after our airport encounter, your mom brought you to MIM after work. I am happy to say, that is the day you and I became friends. I lured you in with my attentiveness and, as any parent knows works best, a couple of games. It was that day you called me "Dad," for the first time since I arrived. What a feeling! In that moment, I felt such a surge of emotion, like I was really, truly your father for the first time. With that one syllable word, you confirmed what I had always known, but perhaps had not yet fully digested yet: You were counting on me, and I had a responsibility to walk you through life; to raise you to become strong enough to persevere through the adversities that, no matter how hard I try to protect you from, I am sure you will encounter.

It was also on that incredible day, I learned about your love of sport (soccer) and music. I never imagined such simple pieces of knowledge could bring such a smile to a man's face, but I suppose I never realized what it is like to get to know what is already one-half of yourself. I noticed you were quick and a fast learner, and I was instantly proud of the potential I knew you already had.

The three hours I had with you went by fast, and then it was time for you and your mom to go back home. I wished you stayed longer, or I went home with you, but I was obligated to fulfill my contract, and more than that, I knew the work I was doing would help me become the type of man who would be better able to show you how to walk in the light with your head held high.

I dragged my feet as I guided you and your mother to the bus station. I frequently paused to kiss you and admire my little son. We waved goodbye and the bus pulled away, carrying with it the two people I love most in the world. I could not move. I was grounded to my spot, weighed down by the unbearable amount I already missed you, although I could still see you in the reflection of the window. My eyes burned with regret at the thought of letting you leave without me. With blurred vision and a broken heart, I headed back to do the work I had been called to do.

THE BEGINNING!

AUTHOR'S NOTE

I began to write this book in a moment of desperation, during the long hot days of 2018. My son, Elvin, was celebrating his second year of birth.

In 2016, I arrived in Canada as a refugee sponsored student at Huron University College. Young and energetic, I was full of hopes and dreams to make it. Entirely determined! But the birth of my son was slowly sending me into deep doubts and guilt and severe reflections of a life and lives left behind. Depression took hold of me in the summer of 2018. His mother, Vumi, would occasionally send me photos of the baby boy. His baby photos were a reminder of my innocent childhood. But mostly, his gaze aroused deep, heartfelt sentiments that forced me to look at the world through his lens. The young adult me constantly interrupted my focus and corrupted my attention, often leading me to elusive interpretations of the world I live in. I had to explain myself. I had to confess to the innocent life I brought in this relentless world. During all these years in the writing, I have tended to think I owe Elvin a confession, and that time is against me.

Just before Thanksgiving of this year, specifically, the night of October 6, 2021, my grandfather (1945– 2021), passed on and was buried in Dzaleka Refugee Camp. I received photos and videos of his burial on WhatsApp. My grandpa's passing was a life-changing and revealing point for me.

In 1994, he left Rwanda for refugee protection in neighboring Tanzania. In 1996, alongside hundred thousands of Rwandan refugees in Tanzania, he was forcibly repatriated to Rwanda. He lived in Rwanda for a while but soon was forced to flee the country for the second time the following year. Encouraged by the UNHCR, the Government of Tanzania, and the new Rwanda government messengers of peace and hope, he returned to Rwanda in 1998.

In 2000, at the threat of his life and security, he fled the country for the third time. He died in Malawi in 2021 as an asylum seeker, with more than uncountable refugee status rejections after twenty-seven years of pleading for refugee protection.

I never felt so connected to him until the last two years of his life. I would call him from the comfort of my home in London, Ontario just to talk. I listened more than I spoke. Our discussions centered on details of his early life as a young man, in Rwanda, and our family history. Perhaps I knew the inevitable was just around the corner. Signs were all around us. He really had prepared us for the impending departure. He lived the last quarter of his life in statelessness only to die weak and desperate. Has he forgiven the world where he rests, peacefully, under unforgiving elements of this world? That I will never know. Not in this flesh, nor in spirit, if spirit is real. How could he lose all he worked very hard to earn for himself and his family during his youthful years, only to die and be buried in exile? How resentful must be our dead?

Now, the passing of my grandfather reminded me of the brutalities of the world I grew up. One that I managed to escape, by twist of fate, leaving an unborn baby forming in his mother's womb. I am haunted at the thought he might inherit the world I left behind.

Run Elvin! is an open letter. The first book in a planned trilogy of my life as a young refugee who immigrated to Canada through good fortune, struggle, and determination. I recall a young life in the crowded, dusty streets of refugee camps, with limited resources and limited hope of a life outside Africa's *open prisons* (refugee camps).

The latest report on child displacement from the United Nations Children's Fund (UNICEF) claims "1 in 3 children living outside their countries of birth are child refugees; for adults, the proportion is less than 1 in 20."[1] I was one of them until 2016.

ACKNOWLEDGMENTS

"Do the best you can until you know better. Then, when you know better, do better."
—Maya Angelou

I am not a good writer.

Ooh yeah! Let that sink in.

This book began in shambles.

---

[1] Source: UNICEF analysis based on Internal Displacement Monitoring Centre (IDMC), Global Internal Displacement Database (GIDD). 2021.https://data.unicef.org/topic/child-migration-and-displacement/displacement/

I am not a good writer. I am glad, I know this. Writing this book has been a humbling experience. My editors understand best. Neither am I the worst writer, nor the first one to walk down the aisle. This book has been my way to learn and practice the craft of writing. And I practiced every single day, at every single opportunity presented to me. I have learned from my editors, plus feedback from family and friends. But largely, I learned a lot through reading different genres of literature. I read and read on! Relentless learning comes to my rescue whenever I fall short. Now, by any means necessary, I am determined to crawl deeper down the rabbit hole. If only I can improve my writing skills at each successful breath.

"Come with me for a ride. You—love the countryside?"

Good music is all I need, plus, a Stella—and a Spadina. Holly ghost—fire! Wait. Maybe not a Spadina.

"Ooh boy!"

Monti should have been here!

"Spadina? Do you miss them?"

I lost my appetite a long time ago. Do you think I should inform my dietitian? The thing is, I have been to these coffee shops, restaurants and bars many more times than I can begin to count. I have had this. Ooh, I had that one too. Now I am learning to cook my own meals, make my own coffee, sometimes smoothies too. The only difference I have learned is the taste. Nothing I make really tastes like any of those. Pity! That's all it has come down to. These days I keep it to myself. I confide in good music. That's how I began monitoring and keeping records of all my cravings. It's my coping mechanism. My way to get back in shape. I keep journals too—all my files are saved on flash drives.

If I can only focus.

Do you see what I mean?

(Story To be continued)

I remember booking an appointment to speak to Dr. Barry Craig, President at Huron University College, about my newfound passion for literature and plans to embark on a writing journey.

Warmly, he welcomed me to meet in his office—to discuss my business project. Writing as an investment. Writing as a business transaction is what it appeared I was going to do. Writing as an art, writing as a lifestyle, writing for the love of writing—that came later after fighting shameless battles with my insecurities.

Nights following my appointment request were spent drafting, putting words and ideas down, like I knew what I was doing. I was only attempting to save myself from shame and humiliation. For days I was confident I had something of substance to present. I went to the school's library to print my early drafts. I would come to learn they were "blueprints" of a "Letter from a Region in My Mind" as in James Baldwin's *The Fire Next Time*. The only difference is that *Run Elvin!* cannot equal any of Baldwin, or Ta-Nehisi's writing. I printed two copies. I used one to practice my presentation and the other was to be handed to Dr. Craig.

I walked confidently into his office with the two copies that really had nothing of substance, but photos depicting my family's genealogy, and the teenage me in Africa. The photos' background and the printed figures said something to me that I couldn't clearly mark out. The only meaning and sense they made to anyone outside of my shoes was: portraits of the I world left behind.

The cover page bore a photo of a young baby boy. Dr. Craig might have assumed it was my baby photo. Now 2018 marked my twenty-fourth birthday. How could he have imagined the baby was my son? He never asked about my selection. I was glad he didn't. Instead, I went into detail about the topics I wanted to cover in the book. He listened eagerly. I had a biblical idea for the book's title. Something along, *Builders and the Rejected Stones*. An appropriately catchy phrase to hook Dr. Craig's interest in my project. Now, the doctor is also an Anglican Priest. He studied Theology. He must know the story of the rejected stone. Having such knowledge should give him a general view of my business project, I thought.

"This will be a very great book, Gabriel." He was very kind.

"Thank you," I said in appreciation.

His belief in my writing endeavors encouraged me to travel back in time; a quest to understand my complicated history.

I left Dr. Craig's office with a dream to become a writer. In ensuing days, a writer, I was becoming. I would claim this project to be a child of a simple idea. The idea that if I walked the walk, if I walked in the shoes of a writer, I would find pieces of me. Traces of me lost along my journey to become this human in me. These pieces would help me to understand my past and the world I come from. The same elements, properly put together, would guide Elvin Gabriel Jr. to whence he came.

Was it necessary to travel this far to encounter the stranger in me?

***

Allow me to acknowledge, Meaghan Blight, Rachel Joanne Macaulay, Dr. Lucas Savino, Dr. Wendy Russell, Dr. Mark Franke, Kristina Stankevich, Lisa Kamenar, Thomas MacVoy, Mary Metcalfe, Dr. Bill Acres, Waseem Kazzah, Dylan Mathews, Tim Day, Alyssa Nunn and her family, and everyone who has been a part of my life's journey as a student, and a new immigrant in Canada.

I would like to thank the student population at Huron for enabling the success of the SRP.

Also, on a very personal note, I would like to thank Elvin's mother for her patience, courage, and strength to care for the boy in my absence.

Finally, my sincere appreciation goes to Nino Pio Ricci, the Canadian novelist. While working on my "Authors Note" and "Acknowledgment," sections of this book, I was overcome with sudden emotions about all the work, time, and people who have helped me to push this project to completion. It is mostly Nino's comments on my early draft that caused me to tear down.

I think Nino's comments on my early draft are significant and encouraging for any up and coming writer, not just me. Nino and I met on November 14th, 2018, during a library event (at Huron University College), titled "LIVING LIBRARY,

MANY PATHS, ONE DESTINATION: Stories of Success in the Pursuit of Passion."

I told him about my love for literature, interest in immigrant stories and experiences, and then I introduced the topic of my book, *Run Elvin!* (then in development). Nino, then working as *Alice Munro Chair for Creativity* at the University of Western Ontario, kindly offered to read through my draft and promised to give me feedback.

His feedback has been the backbone of all my writing.

For the interest and benefit of uninspired generation of young writers, kindly allow me to share Nino Ricci's feedback to early developments of Run Elvin!

Re: Run, Elvin! (Book project, Chapter 3)

Nino Ricci

Thursday 2019-01-19

To: Gabriel Ndayishimiye

Hi, Gabriel.

I read through your chapter and found it very gripping and moving. You clearly have a very compelling story to tell. You have lived through experiences which most of us are only familiar with through the news and thus can barely begin to comprehend. This is a story that should be told and you have clearly been making significant progress in telling it.

I always tell my students that they should regard the early drafts of a project as a way of working out in their own minds exactly what story it is they are trying to tell. As much as we think we know our own story, it is only in the process of grappling with it to put it into words that we begin to discover its deeper aspects. This is true in memoir as much as in fiction. My own early drafts are usually very bad, essentially serving only as roadmaps or blueprints for the story that I will eventually write, having shown me the possibilities of my material as well the aspects of it I haven't yet fully digested. It is only the second or third draft that the real writing begins, because by then I can see a workable shape for the project and have begun to notice underlying patterns in the material. That is always when I truly begin to address issues of structure, language, and style to help ensure the story is presented in its best possible form.

That is a roundabout way of saying that as compelling as your story is, it still feels at an early draft stage. At this point, <u>you should just</u>

<u>worry about finishing the draft to completion</u>. That is very important. Once you have a finished first draft, the hardest part of the job will be done. The rest will just be a matter of going over it and thinking about how you might reshape the material into its most effective form. That might also be a good point to find someone you trust (or several people you trust, and who have some expertise in writing and publishing) to give you some editing advice and assistance.

A few things you might want to think about in your next draft:

- making the chronology of the story clearer. In this chapter, for instance, I sometimes get confused when he is at the camp with his mother, and when with his grandparents. Also, sometimes the story moves backward and forward in time in a way that muddies the chronology.
- making more use of setting. Readers need to see, hear, and feel the world of the story to become immersed in it. Not only that: often setting, and in particular in a story like your own, becomes a crucial way of conveying the meaning of your story. If we can see the refugee camp, we have a much better sense of what it means to spend your life in one.

- use more scenes. Right now, much of the story is coming across in what we call narrative summary rather than in direct scenes. We connect much more directly to direct scenes which seem to unfold in real time, as in a movie. For instance, on page 3, when you leave your mother for another camp, you could give us a much more detailed scene of that event, including the parting from your mother and the voyage to the new camp.
- provide more context when it is necessary for us to understand what is going on. Why are your grandparents in another camp, for instance? How did they get separated from your mother? (Though perhaps you've included this information in earlier chapters.)
- reduce the amount of editorial commentary and analysis you give us. If the story is told fully, readers will reach the conclusions you want them to without your having to spoon-feed them. The main rule in any storytelling is show, don't tell. That is, present the scene and let readers reach their own conclusions. For instance, when you talk about Rodriguez, rather than summarizing your and the other boys' envy of

him, perhaps develop a scene of him and his father more fully that contrasts to your own situation. Readers will then be able to arrive at the conclusion of the longing and envy he inspires on their own.

- reduce the amount of retrospective analysis (this relates to the point above). Right now your adult voice is constantly intruding in the story to tell us how to interpret it. Try to stay more closely to the child's perspective so that we can feel it more deeply.
- If there were a single overall comment I would make that really summarizes all of these suggestions, it would be to trust more to your story to convey its own meaning rather than feeling you have to constantly interpret for us. Often the best way to tell a story is simply to tell it. Start at the beginning and work through to the end, letting its details speak for themselves. That helps ensure that your story has structure (a beginning, middle and end) and helps keep readers interested, since we want to see what happens next. It also helps keep you focused on telling the story clearly and fully rather than worrying about interpreting it for us. Its meaning

will come through with much greater complexity and nuance and feeling in the details of the story than through any retrospective analysis or editorial commentary you can provide.
- I hope that helps. As I say, the important thing right now is simply to push through to the end of the draft. After that, it is just a matter of going back to the beginning and starting again, but now with a better sense of the story you are trying to tell.

Let me know if any of this isn't clear or if you have any questions.

All best,

Nino.

ABOUT THE AUTHOR

Gabriel Ndayishimiye was sponsored to study in Canada through the Student Refugee Program at Huron University College in 2016. He holds a Bachelor of Arts: Honours Specialization in Globalization Studies from Huron at Western University. Currently, he is a part-time student, Master of Arts—Immigration and Settlement Studies program at Ryerson University. Gabriel is also a BIEA-RSC Graduate Attaché, University of Oxford's Refugee Studies Centre (RSC) and the British Institute in Eastern Africa (BIEA).

Manufactured by Amazon.ca
Bolton, ON